DATE DUE

FEB 0 8 2002		
DEC 1 9 2003		
JAN 1 3 2004		
MAY 2 0 2004		
FEB 0 2 2005		
DEC 1 0 2014		
		BP

DEMCO 38-296

MAKING NEWS OF POLICE VIOLENCE

A Comparative Study of Toronto and New York City

JEFFREY IAN ROSS

Foreword by Donna C. Hale

PRAEGER

Westport, Connecticut
London

Library of Congress Cataloging-in-Publication Data

Ross, Jeffrey Ian.
    Making news of police violence : a comparative study of Toronto and New York
City / Jeffrey Ian Ross ; foreword by Donna C. Hale.
        p. cm.
    Includes bibliographical references and index.
    ISBN 0–275–96825–1 (alk. paper)
    1. Police brutality—Public opinion—Case studies. 2. Police in mass media—Case
studies. I. Title.
    HV8141.R67 2000
    363.2'32—dc21   99–054878

British Library Cataloguing in Publication Data is available.

Library of Congress Catalog Card Number: 99–054878
ISBN: 0–275–96825–1

First published in 2000

Praeger Publishers, 88 Post Road West, Westport, CT 06881
An imprint of Greenwood Publishing Group, Inc.
www.praeger.com

Printed in the United States of America

The paper used in this book complies with the
Permanent Paper Standard issued by the National
Information Standards Organization (Z39.48–1984).

10 9 8 7 6 5 4 3 2 1

Dedicated to the victims of police violence
and their families and friends throughout the world.

Contents

Foreword

Making News of Police Violence is useful to scholars, media personnel, police administrators, and perhaps most important, criminal justice instructors and students alike. Building on Jeffrey Ian Ross' dissertation and a series of journal articles and chapters in books, such as his piece "The Role of the Media in the Creation of Public Police Violence," for my co-edited (with Frankie Bailey) *Popular Culture, Crime and Justice* (1998), this book is important because few empirical studies have been conducted on citizens,' governmental, and law enforcement reactions to police use of force. It also places the study of police violence in the context of social problems, communication, public administration, policy, political participation, and social movement research.

Making News of Police Violence is helpful to reporters, broadcasters, and editors who make the daily decisions on which our news of police use of excessive force is based. They may gain a better contextual understanding of the work they do, to see it in a larger framework beyond the daily grind of deadlines, column inches, and seconds that fit. The dissemination of this research may be accomplished by Dr. Ross directly contacting the news personnel, or by his presenting findings from the study at communication/journalism conferences. Cross-professional contacts between academics and practitioners, in this case researchers who study police news reporting and those who practice that reporting, may result in a more thorough understanding of this important news activity.

Findings from this study are advantageous to police administrators and the departments that they lead because they can better understand the dynamic that takes place between news makers and sources. They can also use the media to advertise occasions for citizens to learn what

the police can and cannot do. Recently one of our local police departments advertised the opportunity for citizens to participate in a citizen
police academy. (In fact, this was the third citizen police academy to be
offered in the past several years.) I was a participant in the third 10-week
series.

During one class, when the officers were describing their uniform and
the equipment they use, citizens questioned the police about a recent
incident of deadly force in the community. In their queries to the officers,
the residents referred to what they had read in the local newspaper. By
their questions, the citizens were not challenging the police department;
they just wanted to know how the police made their shoot/don't shoot
decisions. The opportunity to participate in the citizen police academy
provided me with the chance to recognize how public opinion is shaped
by what citizens read in their local newspaper. Throughout the citizen
police academy weekly meetings, police officers answered all questions
professionally and candidly. From my observation of the interactions, it
appeared that the citizens were satisfied with the answers they received.
The citizen police academy provides a forum for police to clarify many
of the misconceptions that citizens possess regarding police work. Police
administrators can use the citizen police academy to improve citizens'
understanding of the roles of police and to explain how the police ac-
complish these roles.

In this citizen police academy class, it was obvious to me that these
citizens' perceptions of police work were influenced by what they read
in the newspaper and saw on television. Therefore, it may benefit the
police department that uses the citizen police academy to begin the initial
session with an exercise designed to ascertain how the public's perception regarding the police is shaped. This exercise may open up channels
of communication between the police and citizens regarding how the
media covers police incidents of violence.

Additionally, the findings from Ross' *Making News of Police Violence*
may stimulate the police department to conduct a short survey with local
residents to find out what activities the citizens believe the police are
responsible for accomplishing in the community. This question may be
followed by one designed to determine how citizens decipher what police are supposed to do (newspaper, television, actual experience, etc.).
In addition, the police may improve police-community relations by
working with the local newspaper to develop a "Chief's Corner,"
whereby the chief would answer different questions the citizens have.

Finally, since I spend a large part of my time teaching undergraduate
and graduate criminal justice management courses, it is here that I find
Making News of Police Violence the most useful. During these classes I
include material describing how media reporting of criminal justice
events influences the perceptions of the public. Also, these courses ad-

dress how media reporting ultimately improves the operations of the criminal justice system. Ross' political process model and methodology may be used to start a dialogue with students regarding the process of police violence. Through this technique, students also learn that media reporting has contributed to changing police policies and practices regarding public disorders. Also, the media has provided the impetus to establish programs designed to improve police-community relations.

Making News of Police Violence may serve as a springboard to introduce students to a panoramic view of the role of the police in public disturbances in America. For example, in the fall of 1998, I taught an honors course with a colleague from the history department on violence in America. One of the topics we covered was the police response to public disorder in American cities. A component of this discussion was the role that the media have in reporting what precipitated the riots, and the actions police used to curtail the violence. A greater part of this discussion focused on the aftermath of the riots. Ross' use of events data analysis and his application of the political process model can augment the students' understanding of recent incidents of public disturbances.

Making News of Police Violence helps instructors discuss with students how in the aftermath of riots the police came under official scrutiny for the way they handled the situations. Instructors can review the history of police and public violence in the United States and explain that after incidents of police violence, commissions were appointed to study why the disturbances occurred and to make recommendations regarding prevention of future police violence.

Generally, criminal justice textbooks only highlight the actions of the police in curtailing public violence in American cities. Usually they cite disturbances including the Election Day riots and the draft riots that occurred during the middle and late nineteenth century in American cities (Fogelson, 1977). Undoubtedly the most unforgettable protests regarding the ultimate changes for the criminal justice system were the Watts and other big-city riots during the middle and late 1960s, as well as the Chicago Democratic Convention (1968).

Instructors may use Ross' case studies of public police violence in Toronto and New York City to stimulate class discussion regarding the media's role in describing more recent examples of police and violence. For example, students can discuss the violence that erupted after the trials of the Los Angeles police officers who were accused of assaulting Rodney King. Alternatively, they may wish to examine recent law enforcement attempts to curtail campus demonstrations against university policies of not using alcohol on campus.

In classroom discussions, however, it is important to emphasize that the police are generally the only organization that is summoned to quell volatile situations in a professional manner. And it is also necessary to stress to students that from the police perspective, the behavior of the public or the "crowd" (as Rudé [1964] referred to public disturbances) is difficult for the police to predict. Although the police have standard operating procedures that they follow to restore peace to the community, they may have to make immediate decisions regarding enforcement measures depending on the behavior of the crowd at the time. Perhaps the more recent examples of the police and public violence reflect how the police have benefitted from the studies of the role and function of police in society, derived from the recommendations of the President's Crime Commission (United States, 1967). Instructors may use this opportunity to introduce or remind students how research is important for criminal justice policy.

Using information from Ross' book may assist instructors when they ask students to recall other episodes where the media played an important role in shaping the public's perception of police violence. Certainly one of the more infamous cases was the Rodney King incident that culminated in the Christopher Commission investigation of the early 1990s. During the fall of 1997, another unforgettable occurrence of police brutality that was covered by the newspapers was the assault on Abner Louima, a Haitian man, by New York City police officers. Situations like this support the reality that reporters are important both to the criminal justice system and to citizens. Journalists not only make the public aware by reporting the news; they also serve as a catalyst that propels these incidents into the public's eye. Ultimately, their coverage improves the operations of the criminal justice system. News coverage is necessary to prevent individual police "rogue" activities from becoming the norm.

When we trace the origins of police professionalism and how the public perceives law enforcement, it is obvious that media coverage of police behavior has played a role. The media's reporting of how the police handle disorder shapes both the public's opinions and attitudes toward the police. The media's coverage has resulted in official examinations of how the police handle public disorders. Ultimately, the contemporary policies and procedures that police departments now utilize have evolved from official examinations of police handling of public disorders. Studies of police performance extending from the Lexow investigation of police brutality in the late nineteenth century to the highly visible Christopher Commission's inquiry of the late twentieth century have changed police behavior by recommending that policing become more professionalized. Studies indicate that this can be accomplished by requiring a college education for police officers, increasing the numbers of women and minority police officers, and providing advanced training for in-service officers. News coverage of police and public violence has contributed to improving the quality of policing and enhancing the image of the police as professionals.

The presence of the media has made the police more accountable to the public it serves. Since the recommendations of the President's Crime Commission in the late 1960s, police administrators and city officials have made concerted efforts to improve the delivery of services and to enhance the public's image of the police. Because of the President's Crime Commission and later police studies, more entry-level positions are presently filled by college graduates. Importantly, the public sees more women and minority officers on the streets. The higher educational standards and inclusiveness of women and minorities have changed the delivery of services and the public's perception of the police.

In the aftermath of public disturbances and police violence, the studies I previously cited recommended that the police become more proactive with the community rather than reactive. One of the most successful methods to achieve this has been community policing. Community policing, beginning in the late 1970s, can be credited today with substantially changing the public's perception of policing and the delivery of police services. Through newspaper coverage of community policing activities and citizens' encounters with police on bicycle and foot patrols, as well as other highly visible crime prevention activities in the community, citizens feel more comfortable with the police presence. The impression they may have once held of the brutal and violent police officer is assuaged by the availability of the community police officer. This new image is enhanced when they read in their local newspapers about the support of community policing by the federal government through the COPS-FAST program. News coverage of community policing has provided citizens with an image of a professional police officer who is there to meet their needs.

However, it must be stated that not all residents trust the police, or even view them as beneficial. Individuals who live in communities where public disorders occur may have less trust in the police and may question whether their presence is useful. Citizen patrols are one method developed by police administrators to involve individuals who question the benefit of police presence in their neighborhoods. The police assist the residents in organizing the citizen patrol operations. The citizens are not involved in apprehension but report all suspicious activities they observe directly to the police for following up. Police administrators need to be aware of ways to improve neighborhood quality of life for residents in high-crime areas. A positive police image results from police and community partnerships.

In conclusion, Jeffrey Ian Ross' research is important on several levels. On a scholarly level, his use of the political process model is a sophisticated tool that helps with the interpretation of episodes of police violence and the media's treatment of law enforcement. Second, Ross' work on the role of media reporting may be helpful to police administrators too. Third, findings from Ross' research, if shared with journalists, newspaper editors, and publishers, may be useful to them. Last, Ross' discussion of media reporting of police violence may be used to dialogue with students regarding how the police and public have benefitted from media coverage.

Donna C. Hale
Shippensburg University

Preface

The names Rodney King, Abner Louima, and Amadou Diallo seem to echo in our minds. They are part of the passing parade of individuals who for one reason or another make their way into the public's consciousness and then slowly fade. Although many people consider excessive police violence disconcerting, if, when, and how they voice their opinion or respond by taking some sort of action is generally unknown. To understand this process, based on a review of the literature and interviews with relevant actors, a four-stage political process model is developed. This model is then applied to the empirical evidence of police violence in two cities, Toronto and New York City, over a 15-year time span. To better focus the study, three well-publicized cases of police violence from each city, matched on important criteria, are the subject of intensive case studies. The study concludes that, in general, most individuals do not respond to police use of excessive force, and if and when they do usually depends on the context of police violence. The research ends with an analysis of the reasons people react so infrequently to police use of excessive violence.

The study addresses a difficult, painful, timely, and important topic for victims, police personnel, and society as well. It presents and tests a theoretical model of public reaction to police use of force. The model integrates a variety of approaches to improve understanding of how communities come to define and control the use of force by police, including but not limited to literature on media effects with that of police violence. Understanding how and under what conditions police violence leads to public and police responses has been understudied. Both quan-

titative and qualitative methods and analysis are used. Tables and figures
are used to enhance the reader's understanding and conceptualization
of issues. The study should be of interest to scholars, practitioners, and
citizens alike.

Acknowledgments

Over the course of researching and writing this book I have incurred a series of debts. Microcomputer difficulties were often solved by Ruy Cabrera. Typed revisions of several drafts of the manuscript were periodically aided by Marie-Christine Cohen and Nichole Pissoneault.

The photocopying of material was provided at various points in time by a veritable army of friends and friends of friends, some of whom included Paul Bond, Henry Brownstein, Joseph Daou, Steven Hughes, Franca Matarozzo, Sam Matheson, Steve Spence, Fern Teodoro, and Steve Wright.

Coordination for the borrowing of library materials not immediately available was aided by Regina Ahram, Anne McCollum, and other staff of the Interlibrary Loan Department and by April Peterson of the Government Documents Section, both at the Norlin Library of the University of Colorado–Boulder. Help with library sources for the Metropolitan Toronto Police Force was aided by Catherine Mathews at the Centre of Criminology Library, University of Toronto. Thanks to all my "sources" who provided invaluable information on which parts of this book are based.

Thanks go also to those who have read the manuscript, in whole or in part, and from whose comments I have benefitted, including Paul Bond, Henry Brownstein, Natasha J. Cabrera, Frank Cullen, Samuel J. Fitch, Ted Robert Gurr, Victor Kappeler, Robert Langworthy, Marie Mark, Otwin Marenin, Reuben Miller, James Schwartz, Lawrence Travis, Kenneth D. Tunnell, and Austin T. Turk. Thanks to Donna C. Hale for an excellent foreword, to Heather Staines, my Acquisitions Editor at

Praeger, for adopting this book, to Marcia Goldstein at Praeger for editorial assistance, and to John Donohue of Rainsford Type for production assistance.

Finally, heartfelt thanks to my wife, Natasha J. Cabrera, who provided an endless source of encouragement and help for every task that this project entailed.

Chapter 1

What Is Public Police Violence?

On May 15, 1979, Rodney Edward Turner, a relatively unknown white drug dealer, accused Metropolitan Toronto Police Force detectives of torturing him by placing a vise grip on his testicles. Turner and his attorney provided information to the Citizens Independent Review of Police Activities (CIRPA), and the resulting investigation led to criminal charges launched against the police officers.

Nine years later, on August 6 and 7, 1988, protesters in Tompkins Square Park in New York City were assaulted by riot police. Approximately 40 white demonstrators were hurt, and four police officers received injuries that required hospital attention. Among the various responses to this incident, the American Civil Liberties Union launched a protest with the Citizens Complaints Review Board, the police chief implemented a retraining program, and a number of senior police officers were transferred.

Three years later, on March 3, 1991, television watchers worldwide viewed the videotape of what seemed like a bizarre ritual of five white Los Angeles police officers brutally kicking and clubbing African American motorist Rodney King. This incident was one of the precipitating causes of the Los Angeles riots.[1]

On April 29, 1992, more than a year after the King beating, the accused officers were acquitted of all charges. The verdict inflamed already strained police-community relations in South Central Los Angeles and incited one of the most violent riots in American history. It eventually spread throughout Los Angeles County and selected cities in the United States. In Los Angeles alone, 4,500 troops and 1,000 riot-trained officers were mobilized, and the three days of riots resulted in 58 deaths, 2,383 injuries, 17,000 arrests, 10,000 fire calls, and $785 million in property damage. All of these totals surpassed the record set by the 1965 Watts disturbances.[2]

As these cases demonstrate, although many acts of police violence/use of excessive force[3] are comparatively similar, the consequences, effects, impacts, implications, responses, and reactions (hereafter outcomes) by the media, community, victims, government, and police (hereafter, community of concern) are probably different. When police engage in violence, it is uncertain whether individuals, groups, and institutions remain passive or press for changes in police departments and the political system. Unfortunately, little is known about the variety of responses to incidents of police use of excessive force.

Research on the process by which incidents of police violence evoke a public outcry and the outcomes of police use of excessive force is necessary for two important reasons. First, the outcomes of police violence are rarely studied. Why? Although a large number of police researchers have devoted considerable resources to study the causes of excessive force, the collection of data on the outcomes of police violence is a Herculean task. Second, expanding our knowledge about the effects of police use of excessive force may help prevent the more extreme forms of political participation (e.g., riots), encourage responsible and responsive municipal political institutions, and minimize the more common response of apathy.[4]

In general, this book describes why some acts of police violence enter the public consciousness, what it is about those events that provokes different reactions, and why concerned actors respond the way they do. For example, when police engage in excessive force, do concerned individuals, groups, and institutions respond by making demands for change from these organizations and the political system by lowering their opinion of the police, or by remaining passive? Coterminously, what causes police violence, how much actual use of excessive force takes place, how do police departments reform after police violence, and how do we control police use of excessive force? These are interesting questions but generally tangential to this study.

An assumption underlying this study is that in advanced industrialized democracies, the police suffer from the "democracy-police conflict," wherein "by the very nature of their function, police are an anomaly in a free society. They are invested with a great deal of authority under a system of government in which authority is reluctantly granted and, when granted, sharply curtailed" (Goldstein, 1977: 1). As such, they are one of the most important government agencies that has the legal right to use violence under prescribed conditions (Bittner, 1970; Klockars, 1985). In particular, it is generally assumed that law enforcement officers engage in more acts of violence than employees of any other governmental organization.[5] This perception is buttressed by an understanding of their working conditions. As street-level bureaucrats, they come into contact with citizens more frequently than actors working for other state coercive agencies.

HOW MUCH POLICE VIOLENCE IS THERE?

Evidence concerning the incidence of police violence is mixed. Because of its controversial and "hidden" nature, it will never be known, with any degree of reliability, the amount, types, and frequency of police violence in any jurisdiction. Thus, in general, events that come to public attention are available for intense scrutiny. There is, however, some recent data that bears on this subject. According to a recent U.S. Department of Justice report (United States, 1997b), "We are now able to estimate, for the first time, the prevalence of all kinds of encounters between the police and members of the public." In 1996, the year during which data was collected, approximately a half-million people had encounters with police. About 500 (1%) of these interactions were estimated to have been warned about a potential use of force or actually had force used against them. Out of this total, however, only 11 individuals claimed to have experienced police violence. If we are to believe this self-reported statistic, at least in recent history, very few people in the United States are victims of police violence. This is not to say that in the past there have been periods during which there was considerable police use of excess force, or that other advanced industrialized countries have more or less police violence. Moreover, when we deconstruct what police violence really signifies, the situation of actual versus perceived levels of police violence is extremely important.

DEFINITIONAL ISSUES

Police violence/excessive force is defined as a type of misconduct, deviance, and police abuse and is used as a generic term for brutality, extra-legal force, riots, torture, shootings, killings, and deadly force.[6] Beyond being a controversial action, however, police violence occurs in a context that is important to the way it is perceived. Indeed, one of the most important perceptually constructed dimensions of police violence is its public/private domain (Ross, 1992a).

The public/private context is rooted in what Torrance (1986: 14–15) calls "public violence." After distinguishing among several types of violence, she focuses on the subcategories of public and private. According to Torrance, public violence "comprises those incidents that are widely regarded as having a significant impact on society or are an important part of it." While admitting that "there is no hard and fast line dividing public from private violence," she suggests that these two types of violence differ on several more or less arbitrary dimensions.

When applying Torrance's distinction to police violence, those acts of police use of excessive force that are detected by the law enforcement hierarchy or civilian actors can be considered public, while those that are not are private. Detection, in the form of officers' notes, citizen/witness complaints, or media reports, has the potential to create public reactions, which make the event public.[7] Unless violent events create negative public reactions, the police have little motivation to change their policies and practices regarding this type of behavior. In fact, it is assumed that sufficient and sustained nonpolice acknowledgment of these acts of police violence plays an important role in law enforcement reform.

Few acts of police violence, however, receive public attention. Among the possible factors that may explain the lack of publicity are the ability of police actors to conceal their activities; victims' decision and/or ability to complain; journalistic/editorial constraints; or dissemination through other formal or informal mediums of communication. In sum, the public/private distinction is important because in order to respond to an issue, the community of concern must first be aware that police violence exists.[8]

LITERATURE REVIEW OF OUTCOMES TO POLICE VIOLENCE

With the exception of attitudinal research, portions of selected government reports, and magazine and newspaper articles, there is little empirical research conducted on the effects of public police violence. Even if such studies were forthcoming, the diverse theoretical literature that could inform this type of study is currently unintegrated, making conceptualization of the problem difficult.

Attitudinal Research

A series of scholarly studies has examined citizens' orientations (e.g., attitudes, beliefs, opinions, perceptions, etc.) toward the police (Biderman et al., 1967; Hahn, 1971; Smith and Hawkins, 1973; Albrecht and Green, 1977; Benson, 1981; Dunham and Alpert, 1988; Brandl et al., 1994). Some of this research has been conducted on nationally representative samples, while other studies have focused on smaller samples of specific races or ethnicities (e.g., Boggs and Galliher, 1975; Scaglion and Condon, 1980, 1981; Mirande, 1981; Carter, 1983; Sullivan et al., 1987). In general, the findings point out that seniors, women, and Caucasians (whites) have a higher regard for police than do African Americans, Hispanics, males, and youths.

Few studies, however, analyze citizens' perceptions of police use of excessive force (e.g., Gamson and McEvoy, 1970; Westley, 1970; Williams, Thomas, and Singh, 1983; Leff, Protess, and Brooks, 1986; Tuch and Weitzer, 1997). Since 1973, the General Social Survey has been used to collect citizens' perceptions of police use of excessive force. This data indicates that educated, white males with incomes greater than $15,000 support police use or limited use of police excessive force. In a review of the literature, Flanagan and Vaughn (1995) suggest that "public opinion may act as a method of social control," and that "different segments of society and incongruous community groups want different kinds of police practices. Individuals who have never had an unsatisfactory encounter with the police are generally supportive of the police or at least ambivalent" and,

if we believe that public perceptions that excessive use of force is common are inaccurate, then efforts are needed to educate the public about the realities of police work and the infrequency of abuse of force. If we believe that these public perceptions are accurate, that they reveal police brutality in the United States as a serious problem, then perhaps organizational and structural changes in the way police agencies conduct their operations are needed. The most likely situation is that both conclusions are valid. (p. 126)

Interesting insights can be gained from a handful of studies that examine citizens' attitudes toward police after critical incidents of police use of force (e.g., Lasley, 1994; Jefferis et al., 1997). Lasley (1994) examines citizens' attitudes as a result of the Rodney King incident. Results from a time-series analysis revealed that the event "adversely" affected people's attitudes toward the police. When the data was analyzed by race, Lasley reported that the incident generated more disdain for the police among African Americans than among Hispanics. Alternatively, Jefferis et al. (1997) look at citizens' attitudes after "critical incidents within local jurisdictions." They report how a widely publicized incident of police violence that took place in Cincinnati in 1995 resulted in a "negative impact on citizens' perceptions of force used by police during arrest situations, but that the effect was substantially greater among non-Caucasians" (p. 381).

Even fewer studies have examined police perceptions of extra-legal force (e.g., Koenig, 1975). Lester (1995), after reviewing the literature on police attitudes toward use of force, concludes that although "the study of attitudes in general and police officer attitudes in particular is [sic] important for advancing understanding of police behavior[,] [a]t present, the study of police attitudes toward the use of excessive force is in only an embryonic stage" (p. 185). Regardless of the sample analyzed, perceptions are usually based on partial information, as many scholars have pointed out. Attitudes sometimes—but not always—may predict behavior.

Portions of Government Reports

Often, in advanced industrialized democracies, after a celebrated incident of police violence, a government inquiry by a commission takes place. Most produce a report. Although these documents comment on citizens' reactions, occasionally they make a series of recommendations to minimize further outbreaks of police use of excessive force. In the United States, some of these reports included those produced by the Wickersham Commission, the President's Commission on Law Enforcement and Administration of Justice, the National Advisory Commission on Civil Disorders (also known as the Kerner Commission), the National Commission on the Causes and Prevention of Violence (headed by Milton Eisenhower), and "Rights in Conflict," the "Advisory Commission on Intergovernmental Relations," the Commission on Civil Rights, and Hearings in New York City on Police Misconduct (also known as the Walker Report), which examined the Chicago riots (United States, 1930–1931, 1967–1968a, 1968b, 1970, 1971, 1981). Most of the recommendations are straightforward and concrete, however, neither do they prescribe guidelines for implementation nor have there been many process or outcomes evaluations of these changes (Kappeler, Sluder, and Alpert, 1998, ch. 8).

The Lack of Theory to Explain the Effects of Public Police Violence

A comprehensive approach to understanding the outcomes of public police violence builds upon a variety of academic literature, including democratic theory, organizational theory, public administration, public policy, evaluation research, political participation, urban politics, social problems, and state theory. Although this book draws from all of this research, in-depth discussions of this work are tangential to conveying the most important theoretical framework (Ross, 1992a).

Even though police violence is interpreted as a "problem," what type of difficulty it is depends on who is labeling it and the possible solutions that are articulated for its resolution. For police departments, use of excessive force is primarily viewed as an organizational, training, or personnel problem. For regulatory/supervisory organizations, police violence is generally a policy or legal problem. Because the issue extends beyond these limited bureaucratic entities, however, police violence is ultimately a public or social problem (Gusfield, 1981). Because of its multidimensionality, police use of excessive force is best viewed as a social problem that incorporates public and governmental concerns.

Unfortunately, scholarly examinations of the reactions to social problems offer limited and incomplete explanations. Henshel (1976, 1990), for example, is primarily concerned with responses to social problems, including intervention, which he describes as "conscious organized efforts to alleviate social problems." He also has a preoccupation with the control or alleviation of social problems. Although Henshel excludes "unconscious or semiconscious means of social control . . . [or] sociocultural developments occurring for reasons entirely extraneous to a given problem,"(1976: 2), he similarly dismisses unorganized responses that can have an effect on social problems (ibid.). Moreover, this approach ignores the possibility that many reactions to social problems are merely symbolic and not intended to have an effect on the so-called "undesirable behavior."

Alternatively, two dominant explanations have emerged that describe the "rise and fall" of social problems. While "natural history" models "trace the progression of a social problem through a sequence of stages" (Hilgartner and Bosk, 1988: 54),[9] "public arena" models "assume that public attention is a scarce resource allocated through competition in a system of public arenas" (p. 55).

With respect to natural history models, Spector and Kituse (1973) develop a four-stage public arenas model whereby "groups assert the existence and offensiveness of some condition," "some official agency responds to the claims," "claims and demands re-emerge expressing dissatisfaction with the official response," and "alternative parallel or counter-institutions are established" (p. 145). And Reissman (1972) produces an alternative natural history model called a "solution cycle of social problems," consisting of three stages: the problem is identified, then it is shaped, and after, in one way or another, it disappears.

Although these perspectives (i.e., natural history or public arena) offer important insights, they are too narrow or simplistic, and neither is satisfactory as a single explanation of social problems. Although proponents of the public arena model criticize "natural history theories for an unrealistic . . . orderly succession of stages" and [for] rarely explor[ing] the competition among other social problems, [they] . . . assume that each [public] arena has an inelastic carrying capacity" (Spector and Kituse, 1973). Unfortunately, both models do not allow for the possibility that individuals and organizations are flexible, and that their ability or motivation to react to social problems varies over time.

Concurrently, social problem research and theory can be divided into objectivism and constructionism (Best, 1989). In sum, objectivists suggest that so-called social problems arise from an objective set of social conditions, while constructionists (e.g., Blumer, 1971; Best, 1989) study how so-called social problems develop in terms of "claims-making," "typification," and so on.

Alternatively, McAdam (1982, ch. 3) proposes, although not especially formulated for the social problem area, a "political process" model whereby outcomes to social problems can be better conceptualized as a series of interactive stages in which power and influence are negotiated among different actors. According to this model, no stage is complete, and actions that occur at each level can have an effect on previous efforts and future actions through a process of anticipated reactions and feedback. I believe that this model is better suited to explain the process of police violence, and with some empirical research, a process model of public police violence can be developed.

SUMMARY

Most acts of police violence never come to the attention of the public, governmental entities, and the wider police department. Of those that do, each act ostensibly has a different effect on concerned constituencies. Having reviewed the definitional aspects of police violence, we can explore more subtle details of what happens after police violence takes place. To specify the effects of police violence, including the role of the media, the political process model is outlined (Chapter 2). Three central questions frame the model: who gets involved, how do they participate, and how do they interact with each other after police violence becomes public? This model describes and explains the typical outcomes of public police violence.

The model is constructed with specific application to police violence, and it may not necessarily be generalizable to other social problems. It is also directed toward large municipal police departments in advanced industrialized democracies. And it is also safe to say that these types of police forces are responsible for providing service to the lion's share of individuals in these types of countries. The process model is a more appropriate alternative to the "natural history" and "public arenas" models.

Specifically, I develop a four-stage political process model that comprises media initiation, arousal, reaction, and outcomes among the community of concern. To empirically test selected hypotheses and subprocesses of the model that are most amenable to verification, I briefly review the history of outcomes to police violence and present descriptive statistics of data derived from newspaper reports on public police violence and analytical case studies of the effects of police violence in Canada and the United States (more specifically, the largest cities in each country: Toronto and New York City, in Chapters 3 and 4).

In the conclusion (Chapter 5), the diverse quantitative and qualitative findings are analyzed and synthesized, and the implications from these results are drawn.

NOTES

1. For a review of the beating and some of the responses to it see David Margolick, "Beating Case Unfolds, as Does Debate on Lawyer," *New York Times*, March 17, 1991; Katherine Bishop, "Police Attacks: Hard Crimes to Uncover, Let Alone Stop," *New York Times*, March 24, 1991, pp. 1E–2E; Robert Reinhold, "Los Angeles Mayor Strives for Calm," *New York Times*, March 31, 1991, p. 14; and Richard Lacayo, "Law and Disorder," *Time*, April 1, 1991, pp. 18–21. Since this chapter was written, Gates voluntarily quit the force.

2. "Understanding the Riots," Part 1, *Los Angeles Times*, May 11, 1992, p. T12.

3. Although I recognize that some scholars would quibble with me, I use the terms "police violence" and "use of excessive force" interchangeably. See the definitional issues section for a more in-depth treatment of these terms.

4. The contentious issue of reforming of police, while important, is beyond the direct scope of this book. My research almost exclusively focuses on the steps leading up to the reform or the lack thereof, which is subsumed by the much broader question of process.

5. This research agenda focuses on physical and not structural violence. For a distinction between the two, see Galtung (1964). Although police can engage in structural violence, physical violence is more visible and easier to measure than structural violence. This study is also restricted to on-duty police use of force only, and it excludes such acts as deaths caused in police chases (see, e.g., Alpert and Fridell, 1992).

6. Thus this field of study excludes police actions against violence and violence against police, and it focuses on violence committed by police. See Sherman (1980) for a distinction among the three.

7. This study is limited to media reports as the catalyst for an event to be considered public police violence. This means of communication should be the most accessible to the community of concern.

8. All future references to police violence and use of excessive force, unless otherwise stated, generally refer to "public" police violence.

9. Some of the natural history models include Fuller and Myers (1941a, 1941b). For a critique of this, see, for example, Lemert (1951). For an extension of this, see Spector and Kituse (1987: ch. 7).

Chapter 2

A Political Process Model
of Public Police Violence

The process by which incidents of police violence come to the attention of the public, government, and police administration, and the resultant reactions by various actors in these constituencies, is complex. With the exception of Pierce's (1986) claim that there is a cyclical nature to outcomes of police violence, little else has been written on this phenomenon. He suggests that awareness of police violence goes through five stages: relative calm, a catalytic police incident, community/political outcry, police sensitivity training, and a return to relative quiescence. Pierce's sequence of steps is, however, too simplistic to describe and to explain such an intricate process, and it lacks empirical evidence to support it. To better explain the pattern, we must develop more sophisticated models and show interactions among the important actors and processes, as well as ordering them in terms of presumed significance. It was with this goal in mind that I developed the political process model. This tool consists of four stages: media initiation, arousal, reaction, and outcomes.

THE PROCESS MODEL[1]

Stage 1: Media Initiation[2]

The publicity that incidents of police violence receive depends, in part, on a series of factors related to the operation of media organizations. A series of studies has been conducted on the media (e.g., Epstein, 1974; Gans, 1979). A smaller subset of that research examined the process by which media organizations make decisions about the types of stories they research, write about, and print or broadcast (e.g., Breed, 1955; Glasgow University Media Group, 1976, 1980; Chibnall, 1977, 1981; Gans, 1979; Fishman, 1980; Ericson et al., 1987, 1989; Rock, 1981; Kasinsky, 1994).

Only a small part of this literature (e.g., Leff, Protess, and Brooks, 1986), however, examines how the media research, write about, print, and broadcast stories on police violence. This is unfortunate, considering that "because [police] are in the media spotlight constantly, [they] are especially vulnerable to having their procedural strays focused upon and controlled through the pressure of publicity" (Ericson, Baranek, and Chan, 1989: 97).

According to police reporters, of paramount importance is the quality of the working relationship between police and journalists. Additionally, the "dynamics of the news production system"—bureaucratic, normative, and economic—must be taken into account (Fishman, 1980: 141–152).

Media initiation is a series of events by which an incident of police violence comes to the attention of news organizations, as well as the decision-making process inside of those bodies, to communicate it to the community of concern. Although the media are seen as the primary agenda setter (e.g., Gitlin, 1980), other institutions and vehicles of communication also play an important role in shaping arousal, reaction, and outcomes. In this policy sphere, social problem, and political relationship, however, the media occupy a central ground for conflict management (i.e., expansion and resolution). The media also serve an educational function, both inside and outside of the police department. For instance, the media might reveal information that may help police managers improve service delivery as well as act as another method for monitoring police employees. Besides affecting the police, news media may also stimulate politicians and activists to respond to problems arising in police-citizen relationships.

It would appear that media initiation, in the form of articles or broadcasts disclosing police violence, depends on a composite of 10 different, interacting factors related to reporters, sources, and news organizations. These variables are ranked in increasing order of predicted importance: gender of reporter(s), experience of reporter(s), number of media outlets in a city, number of reporters, status of reporter(s), source of the report, type of reporters/beats writing/reporting on police violence, kind of news organization, type of medium, and editorial decisions/traditions (Ross, 1998) (see Figure 2.1).

Gender of Reporter

As my interviews (which were conducted with a variety of actors, especially police reporters and public information officers of large city po-

Figure 2.1
Media Initiation

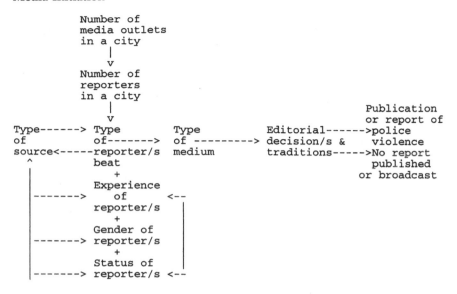

```
         Number of
         media outlets
         in a city
             |
             v
         Number of
         reporters
         in a city                              Publication
             |                                  or report of
             v                                  violence
Type------> Type       Type       Editorial------>police
of              of------->  of --------> decision/s &
source<-----reporter/s medium    traditions----->No report
   ^        beat                                  published
   |          +                                   or broadcast
   |        Experience
-------->      of       <--
   |        reporter/s    |
   |          +           |
   |        Gender of     |
-------->   reporter/s    |
   |          +           |
   |        Status of     |
-------->   reporter/s <--
```

lice departments) indicate, the gender of a reporter can affect the type of information that she or he gathers or has access to. For example, women police reporters are often treated differently than men police reporters; they encounter more difficulty developing sources, and they take longer to do so than do male reporters.

Moreover, many male police officers are paternalistic toward female reporters, and despite the increased numbers of police women in forces, they consider the female reporters "potential dates." In addition to the problems encountered with male police officers, women police reporters also experience discrimination from male reporters, which hampers the free flow of communication.

Experience of Reporter

The greater a reporter's experience in the field and with his or her editors or producers, the higher the likelihood the reporter will uncover stories on police violence and convince editors to publish or air these stories. It takes journalists a long time to master their working environment, to develop expertise in researching and writing, and to gain trust from their sources. Further, the reporter's experience comprises both formal and informal training as well as his or her exposure to different beats. Most reporters learn their trade on the job and get accustomed to their beats through paying a series of visits to numerous and relevant bureaucratic sources (Fishman, 1980: ch. 2). Experience, on the other hand, can in turn influence the reporter's ability to negotiate with his or her editors or producers, to extract information from sources, to determine the amount of time and energy to expend in collecting information for a story, and to better predict the probability that the final product will lead to a published article or an aired story.

Number of Media Outlets

The more media outlets (i.e., newspapers, radio and television stations) there are in a city, the greater the competition among them (e.g., Ericson et al., 1987: 177). As a consequence of this source of stress, reporters may feel pressured to find the most sensationalistic information, some of which will concern police violence. This competitive spirit may also contribute to journalists reporting police violence that is not necessarily excessive.

Number of Reporters

It is also likely that the greater the number of reporters and the higher the competition, the more information will be uncovered. Not only is there external competition (among media outlets), but there might also be internal competition (among reporters inside of media outlets). These processes, in combination, increase the likelihood that reporters will uncover incidents of police violence. Considerable amounts of information, however, do not necessarily translate into printed or broadcasted stories, since there are editorial constraints.

Status of Reporter

News organizations have their own pecking order in terms of whose copy they prefer. According to Tuchman (1978: 24),

the news net is a hierarchical system of information gatherers, and so the status of reporters in the news net may determine whose information is identified as news. Editors prefer stories by salaried reporters to those by stringers, paid less well and on a piecework basis, simply because the news organization has a financial investment in the salaried reporter.

Closely connected to the status of reporters is their experience, because notoriety is usually, but not always, achieved through experience. Columnists, especially those with a celebrity status, are more likely to have their articles published on a regular basis. Similarly, high-status journalists often have easier access to sources difficult to reach.

Source of Report

News of police violence comes to reporters through a variety of sources. In general, these mediums mirror the typical individuals, groups, and mechanisms by which complaints are launched with police departments. Each type of reporter (generally based on the beat he or she covers) depends on a different constellation of sources for his or her news story (Fishman, 1980: 36). In the main, there are two types of sources: written and oral, which may be structured in various ways (Ericson et al., 1987: 42).

Although there are numerous techniques by which sources may "can" their accounts (e.g., press releases) (see, e.g., Ericson et al., 1989: 383), most sources for stories on police violence contact reporters by phone, mail, and fax. Generally, "sources perceive considerable variation among news organizations and respond accordingly" (ibid.). If stories are not heard, published, or aired by the mainstream media, victims can employ a variety of techniques to gain publicity for their plight (Ericson et al., 1989: 313–338). Sources make a variety of decisions about whether and when they will disclose information to reporters. The choice of medium used by sources depends upon a complex array of factors, including speed of transmission and impact as well as their knowledge of which media outlets and reporters are more sympathetic to their situation.

Reporters and Beats

Media reports of police violence come to public attention and are sustained in the public eye primarily by (and in increasing order of importance) the following types of reporters: legislature, court, city hall, and/or police or crime. Different working conditions or beats also determine the reporter's access to sources, the type of relationship (e.g., degree of autonomy) the reporter has with his or her editors, competition among news outlets, and decisions concerning the investigation, writing, and timing of publication or broadcast of articles or segments on police violence (Fishman, 1980; Ericson et al., 1989).

If an incident of police violence does not reach the press through the police, city hall, or court reporters, it might be exposed or sustained through the activities of state or provincial legislative reporters (also known as the press gallery), particularly if the issue concerns a department or ministry such as the Attorney/Solicitor General or Home Office.

In general, more reporters are assigned to cover the police than the courts, however court reporters can be important as gatekeepers in the production of articles or stories on police violence (Ericson et al., 1989: 35). If the police reporter could not report the incident of police violence either because of legal complications (e.g., ban on publication) or because she or he was protecting, or feared "burning" or alienating her or his source(s), the court reporter could do so, for there is a strong possibility that it might not conflict with his or her beat. Predictably, most news stories emanating from the court beat are criminal cases (Rock, 1981; Ericson et al., 1989: 40), and only a few pertain to police violence. Occasionally, however, during a major criminal trial, police violence against defendants, as a by-product of a police investigation or an arrest, is played up by the defense's lawyer.

Occasionally city hall or urban affairs reporters write stories that touch on policing. Often these pieces emanate from the police department itself, or they come to city hall reporters through sources they monitor in various other agencies or departments of city hall. With many of the papers where I conducted interviews, the city hall reporter was formerly a police reporter. This situation increased the likelihood that she or he would have access to police sources and the writing of stories on this subject.

Most stories on police violence, however, are covered by police reporters. The material for these articles or broadcasts comes to police reporters through a variety of different means and sources. The most prominent ways are through community meetings, telephone calls, news conferences, and police occurrence reports. The sources for stories on police violence are either internal to the police force or external to the department. In increasing order of importance, the sources include the police, (including insiders or whistle-blowers in the police force), police radio scanners, the police complaints division, public affairs, the chief's office, organizations and individuals outside of the police department (e.g., the police union or association), police commission members, other reporters, other media outlets, the commissioner of public complaints, the coroner's office, the public prosecutor's office, governmental agencies, concerned members of the community, legal institutions, witnesses at inquiries, established and ad hoc protest groups, witnesses to police violence, independent groups that monitor the police, elected representatives, prominent community leaders, lawyers for victims or their families, the alleged victims' relatives or friends and, most important, the victims themselves, when possible.

A major determinant of access to information from the police is the unique working relationship that reporters have with the police department. The academic literature points to two major types of police reporters: those in the inner circle and those on the outside. Despite the findings of previous research, my sources indicated a complete absence of the insider/outsider distinction or its variance from one news organization or reporter to another (Ross, 1998). Although such a categorization may have been previously appropriate, economic pressures (i.e., budget cuts in newsrooms) seem to have changed this arrangement.

News Organizations

There also is a distinction between popular (e.g., tabloid) versus quality news outlets (e.g., broadsheet) as sources for stories on police violence. As Ericson et al. (1989: 118–119) pointed out, in general, "[p]opular news outlets were oriented to crime-incident reports and primary and tertiary understanding, whereas quality news outlets gave emphasis to policing the police." Further, popular media

are particularly noted for their emphasis on sensational crime, violence, sexual aberrations, major fires, disasters, and other tales of the unexpected that titillate and entertain. "Quality" news outlets, on the other hand, disavow attention to such matters, but this is usually a matter of degree rather than kind. (Voumvakis and Ericson, 1984, as cited in Ericson et al., 1987: 48)

Finally, there also is a difference between mainstream and alternative media. While the former, with mass circulations, publish frequently, the latter cater to a small and select audience and do not publish as often. Also, alternative media are more likely to report stories on police deviance than are the mainstream press.

News Mediums

Even though some writers have suggested that there is little difference among mediums (e.g., Schlesinger, 1978; Tuchman, 1978), others disagree (Glasgow University Media Group, 1976; Graber, 1980; Sheley and Ashkins, 1981). Ericson et al. (1987: 76) say that this discrepancy exists because both groups of researchers have different foci of study. Regardless, media type affects the way that reports of police violence are portrayed (i.e., amount of sensationalism, comprehensiveness, etc.), perception of reliability, and audience.

Newspapers are the most comprehensive type of media that leave a relatively easy retrievable record (generally microfilm and/or indexes) and cover the story in greater depth than other formats. Generally, they are more comprehensive because they have a larger number of reporters in the field than do the broadcast media. This situation often leads to the production of secondary reports by broadcast media, based on the primary research of newspapers. Radio and television, while leaving a permanent record in terms of audiotapes and videotapes, are the most difficult to archivally access. Broadcast media are also more cautious than their counterparts, since their licenses can be revoked by the government for minor violations of federal communications laws. Radio and television, however, are the most effective vehicles for sustaining the personalization and dramatization of a story (Ericson et al., 1989: 214).

Finally, "[t]elevision journalists . . . rely heavily on predictable sources of stories in particular bureaucratic settings" whereas,

newspaper [reporters] ha[ve] more resources, including a greater number of journalists. These resources allow the newspaper to set up a more decentralized system for routine news work, including a larger number and more diverse range of topic and beat specialists. . . . [N]ewspaper time and space constraints are less severe. (Ericson et al., 1987: 354–355)

The popular and quality distinction determines the medium's emphasis on news originating from different beats. Popular formats give the most attention to police beat stories, but there is some indication that broadcast news is increasingly seeking out these stories (Ericson et al., 1989: 393–394). As with different types of organizations, each kind of source is attracted to alternative mediums. Finally, every organization can marshal varying and different resources to cover a particular story.

Editorial Decisions and Traditions

In addition to the relationship between reporters and sources, a complex understanding exists between journalists and their various editors or producers. This interaction affects the assigning, researching, writing, editing, and printing or broadcast of articles or stories on police violence. Many of these decisions occur in newspaper, radio, and television newsrooms, reflecting their unique agendas and economic constraints.

In deciding if, how, and when a story will be run, most editors or producers (as well as reporters) make decisions about the reliability and "abnormality" of the piece, its sources, other competing articles that they deem newsworthy, and other stories that are on schedule, or were written or shot for that day's news. Also of concern are the ramifications of the piece as well as the predicted energy necessary to substantiate the claims and complete it. Some of these decisions evolve from an attitude of self-censorship, that is, the avoidance of controversial stories by editors and journalists. Many of these editorial decisions are related to what is generally referred to as aspects of occupational newsroom culture.

These decisions are made in two contexts (i.e., two points where editors exercise control): before a story is written or shot, and once the story is written or shot (e.g., Glasgow University Media Group, 1976, 1980; Schlesinger, 1978; Tuchman, 1978: 31–38; Burns, 1979; Fishman, 1980; Ericson et al., 1987: ch. 6; Ericson et al., 1989).

Editorial decisions will ultimately determine if a segment will be broadcast or an article published that mentions police violence. They also affect the tone and/or treatment of that report. Although the publication of an article or the broadcast of a report of police violence inevitably leads to public, governmental, and police arousal, the media act as a catalyst and filter through which competing definitions and interpretations are channeled. They can also create resolution or can further excite constituencies by what is not reported.

Stage 2: Arousal[3]

Arousal refers to the extent, intensity, and perception created by "news" of police violence. It concerns both the factors surrounding the report of police violence and the people and constituencies that respond. Although individuals may act on their own, arousal occurs largely in the context of a group. Each constituency in the "community of concern" is affected differently, with varying degrees of intensity. Their perception of the incident(s) of police violence is largely dependent, first, on a number of background factors and, second, on the actions of other concerned actors.

Arousal serves a number of functions. It is a means of increasing group solidarity, a route to achieve publicity for secondary issues, a method for group elites to posture, and a way to reinforce citizens' feelings that they have a measure of control over government. Most important, arousal is a catalyst for reaction in the police department, which affects the control initiatives the police take, the resistance they put up, and/or the public relations measures they engage in.

Episode Characteristics

Three categories of episode characteristics are hypothesized to affect the community of concern's arousal to police violence: victims' characteristics, type of police violence, and rate of police violence. Initially, victims' characteristics sometimes help the public identify and empathize with them. For example, the *race and ethnicity* of some victims have been noted to have an effect on police treatment of suspects (Black and Reiss, 1967; Black, 1970).

In particular, visible minorities and those not speaking the dominant language of the country are singled out for more violence. Similarly, if the victim of police violence belongs to a politically vocal visible minority group, there could be some form of public protest against the police action (Weitzer, 1996). Likewise, the *gender* of the victim can also be a factor, particularly if the victim is a woman and is perceived as physically powerless against a male police officer (Kraska and Kappeler, 1995). Closely related to race and gender, a victim's *stature* could also have an effect on arousal.

If the person is a well-known figure (e.g., a respected member of the community or an infamous person, such as a notorious criminal), or if the general community can identify with that individual, then there is likely to be concern from members of the public. Moreover, the victim's *age* could be important if it contributes to the perception that he or she was physically defenseless during the confrontation. For example, children, juveniles, and the elderly are thought to be physically weak in comparison to police officers (Kappeler, Blumberg, and Potter, 1996: chs. 3, 5).

The *demeanor* of the victim, particularly if he or she is perceived as overly intoxicated, high on drugs, mentally ill, physically disabled, or otherwise easily controlled, can cause a public uproar if it is believed that the police used excessive force against such a person (see, e.g., Kappeler, Sluder, and Alpert, 1994: ch. 6). Additionally, the physical *size* of the victim, judged in relationship to that of the police officer committing the violence, could arouse sympathy if the victim is smaller in size than the police officer. Related to size and demeanor is the *activity level* of the subject. If the victim was *passive* during the interaction (e.g., cooperating) or was conversely *active* (e.g., running away, resisting, or carrying a weapon), it could impact on the audience's perception of the event.

If the circumstances surrounding the issue are *moral or controversial* (e.g., protesters blocking an abortion clinic who are arrested and who then charge the police with brutality), the event has a high likelihood of arousal. Moreover, if the *number* of police involved in the incident is greater than the number of victims, additional empathy toward the victims is aroused. Furthermore, a *similar situation* occurring in a neighboring jurisdiction can affect the response of the community of concern in another.

More important, the more severe the primary type of police violence, the greater the likelihood that the community of concern will react. In many respects, this may instigate a moral panic (e.g., Gusfield, 1963; Hall et al., 1978) or a scandal (e.g., Sherman, 1978). Closely connected to the type of police violence is the public's perception or official judgment that the events caused by the officers were *illegal*. If illegal, the legitimacy of the police is called into question, which could in turn increase arousal.

The chain reaction that questionable police legitimacy provokes may be heightened when *legal sanctions* are applied to the offending police officers or police departments, particularly when the officer(s) are convicted of an offense, or the police officer(s) or department(s) are ordered to make financial restitution to the victim or the victim's family. Legal sanctions subsume the actions of judges, justices, crowns, juries, grand juries, district attorneys, and prosecutors. Such actions include the court's consideration of which law applies to the case, investigating criminal allegation(s), filing a charge, convicting officer(s) of all or some of the charges, and sentencing police.

There also could be a threshold (norm) of the amount and type of police violence that is tolerable, which would determine when and how police departments, communities, and the government respond. For instance, the amount of *previous police violence* that a community has experienced, or for which the police department has been criticized, may serve as a catalyst for the community of concern to be aroused and to respond accordingly.

Similarly, the *perception of previous police violence* is perhaps more important than the actual amount of previous police violence (which is usually unknown). The amount and type of media coverage, the accessibility of the reports (e.g., through a news index), the placement of stories (page number and position on page or order in a newscast), whether out-of-town media outlets pick up the items, the number of different organizations that express concern and demand action, and the way in which these organizations behave are all contributing factors affecting the intensity of arousal.

Finally, and most important, similar to the process involved with media selection of stories, the types of police violence receiving the greatest attention, in predicted ascending order of *severity*, are brutality (unspecified), assaults, beatings, torture, riots, shootings, and killings (unspecified). In sum, episode characteristics are interactive. There is an intimate connection both among them and the actors who are aroused by the event.

Actors/Type of Group

Three types of audiences or constituencies can respond to police violence: the public, the government or bureaucracy, and the police.[4] Ostensibly, each organization has its own interpretation of an incident and/or a problem of police violence, and consequently, of the suitable responses, approaching what may be characterized as the maximization postulate (Lasswell, 1971). Since these actors' decisions should affect the intensity and duration of arousal, their perceptual understanding of police violence is of prime concern.

Public (Members of the Public and Public Organizations)

Six kinds of public can be aroused by police violence. First, and probably least significant, are *prominent police research and interest organizations* such as the International Association of Chiefs of Police, the Police Foundation, the Police Executive Research Forum, or the Canadian Association of Chiefs of Police. Their arousal is dependent upon their organizational mission, which can include research and/or advocacy.

Second are *businesses and their associations*, including legal, illegal, mainstream, and marginal types, which generally ignore issues of police violence. However, police use of excessive force can encourage gossip, position taking, and posturing in support of the police, especially if a great deal of a business' revenue depends on officers' financial support (e.g., restaurants, bars, dry cleaners, manufacturers, etc.). Alternatively, gossip that is critical of the police can be fostered if businesses feel that they have been singled out for police harassment (e.g., prostitutes, massage parlors, cab drivers, street vendors, etc.).

Third are organizations such as *police unions or associations*, which ostensibly work in the best interests of their members (Evans, 1972; Hervey and Feuiile, 1973; Levi, 1977; Reiner, 1981). Consequently, they engage in a variety of activities that are designed to protect the officers that they represent from police department charges and policies.

Fourth are *citizen groups or organizations and leaders* that often serve as catalysts for issues to gain public attention, particularly if a member they represent is affected by police violence. This subsumes the actions of ad hoc or established, community, interest, minority, political, pressure, protest, professional (pro- and anti-police) groups, religious groups and organizations, members of government (including political parties, opposition, or out of power), prominent, fringe, and opinion leaders, professional experts, and academics (see, e.g., Barak, 1988).

Fifth, if the event comes to the attention of the *media*, whether they have published or aired the initial story, a complex chain of events ensues. The media can treat the event as an everyday occurrence and can ignore it, or they can assign reporters to investigate the claims, thus sustaining the issue. Generally, this process can involve many of the components previously mentioned under media initiation.

Finally, and most important, the alleged or actual *victim* (if he or she is still alive) and/or *relatives or friends* of the victim can bring the action of police violence to the attention of the community of concern.

Government/Bureaucracy

Eventually, *government agencies*, at various levels, learn about acts of police violence. The Police Commission, Ombudsmen, Commissioner of Public Complaints (if one exists), the Federal Bureau of Investigation (FBI), Solicitor/Attorney General, the public or civil service commissions, ongoing inquiries into the police, and the justice/department/agency monitor these events and are often responsible for investigating or offering of explanations to other actors in the system.

In particular, *courts* (at various levels, including the actions by judges, juries, and prosecutors or district attorneys) become involved if the issue may or actually does result in a criminal charge or a civil suit being lodged against a police officer or department. Prosecutors consult with judges, the plaintiff's lawyer, and police force officials when assessing whether criminal charges should be brought against the police officers.

Additionally, *appointed officials* at the municipal (e.g., city managers, some city council members, police board members, and commissioners), state or provincial (e.g., Attorney/Solicitor Generals, Ombudsmen), and federal levels (e.g., senators, Attorney/Solicitor Generals, if appointed) take an interest in the situation if it affects their job or if questioned for comment by the media, community groups, or researchers.

Moreover, *elected officials*, including members of government at the national/federal (senate or legislature), provincial/state, and municipal levels (opposition or otherwise), most mayors, and some police executives (i.e., sheriffs) are considered public representatives, since their positions were achieved by voters' choice. They become involved in the aftermath of actions of police violence if it affects their job or constituency, if they are contacted by the media, or if they perceive that there is an opportunity to promote their reelection prospects and/or to undermine someone else's efforts.

Police

Both the accused *officers* and the *senior management* in the police department can become aware of police violence. Typically, the supervising officer receives the accused officer's report and sometimes the head of internal affairs obtains it as well. Occasionally, details of the incident may reach public affairs and the office of the chief of police.

In general, five kinds of arousal to police violence are encountered: denial, doubt, indignation, surprise, and acceptance. These are not exclusive or successive responses to the news of police violence, but they can occur repeatedly and in combination as information concerning an event is made public. Undoubtedly, only certain episode characteristics are important. Furthermore, it is predicted that the greater the number of relevant episode characteristics, the higher the number of groups that are affected, thus the greater the intensity and duration of arousal by the three categories of actors (see Figure 2.2).

Stage 3: Reaction

The reaction of each actor represents the next stage in the political process model. Whereas arousal deals with the perception of the event, reaction reflects the behavior of the community of concern in the wake of arousal. Each individual and group potentially responds differently to the news of police violence. The reaction can be conceptualized as a multistage process.

First, an actor's response can be characterized as one of four types of reaction to be classified, in increasing degree of effort expended, as avoidance,[5] analysis, advocacy,[6] and public relations, with the understanding that the first three behaviors can serve a public relations pur-

Figure 2.2
Arousal

```
Initial
media        Episode            Type of                    Intensity
report +     characteristics +  actor/s and ----->         and duration
of                              their perception/s          of arousal
police
violence
```

pose.[7] Subsequently, each of these responses can be broken down into three successive substages: evaluation, decision, and, if change is recommended, implementation.[8] Depending on the relationship of the actor to the police, the former either criticizes, supports, and/or seeks remedies from the police.

The police department, in turn, usually "does something" to maintain or enhance its legitimacy with the other actors in the respective political and bureaucratic system(s). Indeed, as civil servants who are publicly accountable, police rarely refrain from responding. As in the arousal stage, the participants can be motivated by a number of episode characteristics and organizational factors (e.g., issue attention span, type and numbers of members, finances, mandate, relationship with other agencies, etc.). Although there may be genuine interest in the specific incident of police violence, the situation may also serve as a vehicle to promote each actor's mandate. Regardless, the reaction usually acts as a catalyst for the process of negotiation and the outcomes.

Public

Initially but least relevant are the reactions of private businesses. Should they support the police, these actors might individually or collectively engage in advocacy in a number of ways, including sending a letter to the editor of a newspaper, taking out a display ad in a relevant publication, purchasing radio or television time pledging support, or helping sponsor a "Cops Are Tops" program or event. Often this activity is in conjunction with (if not directed by) the police association or union.

On the other hand, support for the police might be withdrawn by refusing officers discounts on purchases or services rendered, or by acting discourteously toward them. Similarly, an insurance company may threaten to cancel or actually cancel the policy on a police department due to increased losses from suits launched by plaintiffs as a result of police violence.

Nationally recognized police research and interest organizations may provide research support to police departments and government agencies that implement various police-related programs. Generally, their reactions are restricted to conducting research, disseminating reports, publishing newsletters or journals, and serving as credible and regular sources for the media.

Police associations' or unions' initial reaction may be one of avoidance, followed by self-analysis, public relations, and then advocacy. They try to mitigate police department change that may negatively affect their membership or lobby for policy changes that their constituency desires. Police associations and unions usually come to the aid and defense of the accused officers, especially if they are thought to be wrongfully dismissed.

Besides these functions, police associations may file grievances, press for regularizing discipline procedures, minimize ad hoc punishment, limit certain kinds of punishment, threaten to sue or sue the police department or city, promote after-hour contacts between the police and the public, or present the police's interpretation of the incident(s) through their official publication or the press. Although most of their activities replicate those of citizens' organizations, the police union is generally better financed and organized than most community groups, and it can sustain long-term advocacy and public relations more easily. They also have more experience, expertise, and political influence, and thus they can muster a considerable amount of public support (e.g., Evans, 1972; Gammage and Sachs, 1972; Ruchelman, 1973, 1974; Levi, 1977; Reiner, 1985).

Community groups and leaders generally engage in advocacy. They employ the same strategies and techniques used by victims, their relatives and friends, and police unions or associations, with the added strength (in some cases) of having more constituents. In particular, they can form or mobilize to make demands on authorities, organize and participate in public demonstrations, initiate petitions, and so on (e.g., Woliver, 1986; Zald and McCarthy, 1988).

The media also can engage in the full range of reactions. For example, reporters or editors can simply ignore information on police violence. More typically, though, the media can assign a reporter to either write or shoot a "matching" or follow-up story, or write or shoot a series of postured or actual investigative journalism pieces. Other possible reactions include the production of news analysis segments, the solicitation, writing or shooting, and printing or airing of op-ed pieces, or writing editorials that either condemn or favor the police, community, or governmental actions. Editors or reporters might also write rebuttals to letters to the editor that their news organization has published.

More important, the victims and their friends or relatives can engage in advocacy. In particular, they may register their complaint with a variety of actors (e.g., the media, police, Ombudsmen, Solicitor/Attorney General, their elected representative, etc.). They may publicize their plight by writing letters to the editor of newspapers, paying for advertisements, or holding one or several press conferences. Through these mediums, they may demand an investigation; a dismissal of particular officers; the resignation of the police chief; or that certain reforms be implemented in the police department, Police Complaints Division of a police organization, the Police Commission, or the Civilian Review Board (CRB).

They also may hire a lawyer who can sue or threaten to sue the police, or engage in other legal actions. If the victims, friends, or their families are not satisfied with the responses of official bodies, other types of charges can be laid against the police. This becomes a particularly complicated process when charges concerning the denial of civil liberties have been laid. A civil rights case may take decades to adjudicate.

Government/Bureaucracy

Government agencies also can engage in the full range of reactions. These include a variety of investigations by different bodies (e.g., Police Commission, FBI, district attorney's office, justice department or agency, etc.), the establishment of a Royal Commission/Senate Inquiry, the firing of the Police Chief, and, in extreme cases, the suspension of the entire police force.[9] Actions by government agencies may also prevent community advocacy from having any effect on the outcomes (e.g., Zimmring and Hawkins, 1971; Turk, 1976; Handler, 1978; Zemans, 1983; and Woliver, 1986). This obstruction includes enacting special legislation, banning public demonstrations, marches and rallies, and so on (Marx, 1981).

Additionally, if the incident makes its way to the courts, the actions of government agencies usually involve analysis or advocacy. The courts' actions include decisions imposed by judges, justices, crowns, juries, and prosecutors or district attorneys. Only if court orders are ignored by the police or other actors can the court advocate. For example, court responses in support of police officers can nullify or exacerbate reactions by other actors in the community of concern. Such court decisions may result after a ruling that the police violence was within legal boundaries, or that insufficient evidence was marshaled by the plaintiff, defense, or prosecution. If this takes place, the police officer's actions are considered legal. This group of court actions, termed *legal clearance*, covers acquitting, suspending prison terms, granting bail, upholding acquittals, and striking down lower court rulings on the sentences of officers.

Moreover, appointed officials' reactions can include the full spectrum of actions depending on the relevance of police actions to their legislated or perceived mandate. These individuals can launch a departmental inquiry, speak to the media, or resign from their jobs to reflect a real, perceived, or postured loss of public confidence in their ability.

Finally, elected members of government may use the incident to call for reforms, take positions, or claim credit. Mostly, they engage in the full range of reactions. In particular, they can make their views public (e.g., contact a police reporter, ask the bureaucracies they manage to investigate the matter, or persuade others (e.g., the mayor, the Police Chief, Commissioner, Sheriff, Public Safety Director, etc.) to intercede or investigate the matter on behalf of a constituent or constituency.

Police

Accused officers generally engage in some form of advocacy or public relations on their own behalf (Waegel, 1984). Those accused of violence may participate in face-saving actions, both inside and outside of the department (see, e.g., Goffman, 1959; Edelman, 1964; Manning, 1971; Box and Russel, 1975; Christensen, Schmidt, and Henderson, 1982). In addition to engaging in everyday public relations (e.g., rationalizations) with their supervisors, peers, and families, they might initiate letter-writing campaigns, hire a private lawyer, utilize a police union lawyer, trade information, increase the number of tickets they issue or arrests they make, and appeal departmental decisions. Moreover, they may increase, or draw attention to, their work record, community work, and/or sue the police force, victims, or their supporters.

The most common reaction by the police department is the analysis of the incident. This stage can involve the investigation of the incident, the production of an internal report, the establishment or meeting of internal review or disciplinary committees, and/or the formation of joint citizen-police committees (if they do not already exist). The investigation can serve as a means of analyzing both the incident of police violence and public relations.

In the main, police departments may start a two-stage process when they learn of accusations of police violence: an initial criminal investigation, followed by a departmental inquiry. In the event of a possible criminal indictment, cases may be forwarded to the district attorney's office for further investigation and possible action.

Avoidance, analysis, advocacy, and public relations can stimulate public, governmental, or other police reactions. If the public perceives that the police are stonewalling, they can pursue a variety of strategies (e.g., write letters to the editor of the local newspaper or broadcast news organization, calling for an independent investigation, etc.). Public relations efforts by the police might pacify an aggressive public. But public protest, particularly if violent, may stimulate further violence by the police. Any of the four reactions may foster another type of reaction. For example, initial avoidance by the police may be superceded by public relations, if the police organization believes that the first response was inappropriate or insufficient (see Figure 2.3).

Figure 2.3
Reaction

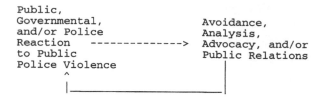

Stage 4: Outcomes

Outcomes is the most complicated of the four stages. In general, it is the final result of the exchange or maintenance of influence or power through a process of formal and/or informal negotiation among the concerned actors to ostensibly resolve the situation. It could be said that the process has two logical outcomes: change and stability. However, even avoidance and public relations may lead to subtle organizational change. For example, they might affect the way in which concerned actors react the next time to news of police violence.

The police department is at the center of this process, and how it reacts strongly influences present and future acts of police violence and police-governmental public relations (Gamson, 1968: ch. 6; Duncan, 1972). Furthermore, police department responses can be ordered along a continuum of "tangible" versus "symbolic" actions (e.g., Lipsky, 1968: 1152; Fainstein and Fainstein, 1974: 193). Firing an officer would be an example of a "tangible" process (e.g., Gusfield, 1963; Edelman, 1964, 1971), while holding a press conference would be considered a symbolic event. The distinction between tangible and symbolic actions is difficult, because tangible actions carry with them symbolic benefits as well (see, e.g., Wilson, 1973).

The most socially relevant outcome to the community of concern is control (Gibbs, 1989). Essentially there are two potentially complementary principal outcomes for police departments: external and internal control initiatives (Hudson, 1972; Tifft, 1975). Although it was acknowledged in the reaction stage that the police can engage in avoidance or public relations, resistance (which is similar to avoidance) and public relations are used differently in the context of efforts that demand changes in control.

In the long run, *external control initiatives* (e.g., *Police Act*) that demand, impose, or legislate more control in and of the police department are met with three possible responses by the police force: resistance, public relations, and internal controls. External controls are limited in scope and impact. First, the day-to-day activities of patrol officers are generally unaffected, since most police are mobile, lack continuous supervision, work within a sympathetic subculture, and are suspicious of outsiders (see, e.g., Becker, 1963; Kappeler, Sluder, and Alpert, 1998, chs. 3 and 4). Second, police actions to solve the problem of police violence are generally inadequate, because insufficient resources are allocated to the problem. Third, the controls are generally flawed, because they are informed by poor research. Fourth, the policy recommendations tend to be impractical or to lack clear goals. Fifth, there may be failures in the implementation of the new policies (Hening et al., 1977). Sixth, police administrators interpret external controls as threats to their power, and consequently they are reluctant to implement them. Seventh, even those changes that are implemented are often symbolic (Manning, 1971). Eighth, many police administrators have poor managerial skills (Punch, 1983, preface). Finally, decisions are often made in a partisan political context, where expedience is more important than long-term effects. In sum, police policies are either inadequate, flawed, lack clear goals, or are, in most cases, merely symbolic.

Additionally, how policies and practices are implemented depends on who is responsible for administering the change (Murphy, 1977: 23). Outsiders to the police department (e.g., District Attorney offices, reform police chiefs, etc.) are particularly effective if they have developed a trusting relationship with the police, thus they can "clean house" quickly. Regardless of who implements them, external controls can only be revised incrementally. Nevertheless, regarding reports by external bodies, while some recommendations are eventually implemented, there is commonly a significant time lag between the policy change and its implementation. Thus senior police management constantly deals with the accumulated recommendations of the community's various constituencies.

Besides external controls, two parallel processes may be operating: resistance and public relations. *Resistance* consists of the conscious or unconscious blockage by police of demands by the public and government regarding change in policies and practices in the police department. Police departments, like other organizations facing a crisis, may respond defensively and rigidly and experience internal conflict (see, e.g., Watson, 1967; Niederhoffer, 1969: 13; Fink et al., 1971). It is difficult for organizations to share or relinquish their power with other groups. Alternatively, many changes increase the financial burdens already placed on resource-strapped departments. A defensive reaction by police may involve the Police Chief writing a letter to other governmental agencies, or a newspaper explaining why the Police Chief will ignore certain mandates, providing recommendations and/or justifying his or her organization's position. Police stonewalling the implementation of new regulations is also a common practice.

Additionally, the police may engage in overt expressions of dissent, sometimes in a violent fashion (e.g., strikes or riots). Much of this behavior depends on the degree of autonomy the police organization has (see, e.g., Johnson, 1981: 189; Marenin, 1990). Resistance also may be combined with public relations efforts. For example, police departments may try to use the police association to stir up public discontent with the external policy recommendation. Such actions often lead to external arousal, which in turn again initiates the whole process of negotiation.

Public relations actions, at this stage, employ symbols and myths to counter governmental external control initiatives. These public relations practices include continued posturing, such as the introduction of vague policies and practices, minimizing or making light of the severity of the events, blaming the victim, criminally charging the victim, suggesting a "bad-apple" explanation for the officer(s) in question, releasing sketchy reports on the violent event(s), agreeing to reorganization, co-optation, or creating new rules and regulations (Murphy, 1977: 33).

Other practices involve having departments investigate similar problems, gaining media attention for their ability to combat crime, the increasing use of community relations programs and/or policing to improve or restore favorable images of the police (Ross, 1995a, 1995b), minimizing the perception of the officer's guilt to prevent a criminal charge from being laid, and/or hampering the successful prosecution of a case. Specifically, police public relations actions consist of lifting the suspension on an officer, terminating an investigation, dismissing a departmental charge, rejecting a complaint, submitting letters to the editor of a newspaper or magazine, publicizing the agency's ability to combat crime, refusing to answer reporters' questions, censoring reporters whom they normally would not, and holding a press conference to present their side of the story. The police also can solicit the support of various pro-police community organizations, such as the police association or the Police Athletic League.

Public relations is commonly carried out through the Police Chief's office, Public Affairs, or police conduits such as the Police Athletic League, police or community crime prevention division/department, and favorable insider police reporters (Radelet, 1977; Beare, 1987; Garner, 1987). Rather than resolving the initial problem, public relations temporarily diverts attention from the specific incident(s) of police violence. Most of the programs that will effect genuine changes are not introduced.

In short, the event that led to the crisis of legitimacy is ignored, forgotten, or inadequately addressed. If the problem of police violence was solved through external controls, it would lead to a reduction in the police's ability (i.e., power) to exercise independent control over their organization. Consequently, public relations is a method that police use to maintain and advance their organizational interests (Reiner, 1983: 145). Moreover, public relations efforts may generate external complacency or increased agitation but will not change police policies.

The introduction, resurrection, and implementation of different and "realistic" *internal control initiatives* are hypothesized to be the most important organizational factor affecting the amount of police violence (see, e.g., Fyfe, 1988). Not only do internal control initiatives comprise the most complex process in the outcomes stage, but they are also difficult to detect by outsiders. Internal control initiatives are the police's own methods to minimize future acts of police violence. It is hypothesized that the police are more amenable to the implementation of their own internal controls than they are to introducing—in whole or in part—external controls. These internal controls give the police department the power to interpret the problem and put their stamp of approval on the changes that the organization produces. Internal control initiatives usually originate with the Chief of Police or go out under the Chief's signature.

It is expected that controls initiated from inside the police department will carry more weight than those implemented from outside. And those controls directed against *individual* officers will be more effective than those involving the *entire* police establishment (Lundman, 1979). By the same token, there are a number of organizational impediments to internal controls (Reuss-Ianni, 1984: 91).

Regardless, police departments implement internal controls because of organizational growth, the presence of reform-oriented police chiefs brought in from the outside, and, most important, in this context, critical events (Sherman, 1978, 1983). First, organizational growth may lead to the development of separate units, some of which are responsible for monitoring the legal and ethical integrity of the institution (e.g., Internal Affairs). Second, at least in the area of police corruption control, Police Chiefs, who are hired externally with a mandate of "cleaning house," and who owe very few favors, can change police departments more effectively than those who have ascended through the ranks. Finally, "critical events" such as police violence may stimulate change. However, not all incidents of police use of excessive force which become public reach the status of critical events. Even if an incident does receive this characterization, it may not engender organizational change (Sherman, 1983: 124).

Examples of internal control initiatives against the *entire* police force include changes in supervision and reporting. First, new supervisory bodies and policies inside the force may be established, such as an internal affairs and/or a public complaints department (if one does not already exist), an automatic evaluation of police officers' actions by internal review committees, transfers, immediate suspension or temporary leave, automatic visits to the force's psychologist, and the banning or revision of guidelines on the use of certain controversial practices (e.g., choke holds, stun guns, etc.). Second, there may be changes in reporting requirements (e.g., directly to the Chief, firing gun, use of force, etc.).

Internal control initiatives against the entire police department gen-

Figure 2.4
Outcomes

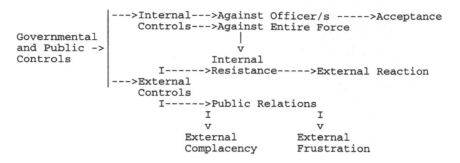

erally prompt officers to better conceal their deviant behavior and/or to set into motion the same processes as those initiated when external controls are resisted. Further, internal controls directed against the entire organization may stimulate the police union or association, which may protest on behalf of the police force.

Internal control initiatives against *individual* officers (i.e., administrative/disciplinary) may consist of reprimanding, retraining, demoting, transferring, reassigning, suspending, fining, firing, and/or criminally charging an officer.[10] Internal mechanisms against individual officers should be better accepted than internal measures affecting the entire organization. As is true for internal controls directed against the whole organization, actions against individual police officers can involve the police association.

Finally, rarely mentioned but nevertheless important is the fact that "it is much easier for a cop [than a citizen] to get back at another cop for a real or supposed wrong within that [informal] system. Since the civilian is outside the system it is impossible to use its social sanctions against him" (Reuss-Ianni, 1984: 101). Punch (1983: 237) finds that at least in the area of corruption, "[p]olicemen who gratuitously broke the code of silence (as opposed to those who excusably 'coughed' under investigation), witnesses, and investigating officers were exposed to informal social control from colleagues in the form of physical threats, blackmail, and ostracism."

If officers are receptive to control initiatives that are both realistic and adequately implemented, there is a high probability that police violence will be reduced. If there is resistance, however, the problem persists, and it may even worsen. Ironically, public relations may either calm some of the public and the government and/or increase their frustration (see Figure 2.4).

Factors such as media initiation, community, government, and police arousal and reactions prompted by police violence should affect the

Figure 2.5
An Outline of the Process Model

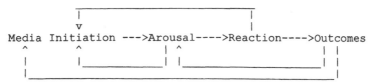

```
                  |_____|
                  |                       |
                  v                       |
   Media Initiation --->Arousal---->Reaction---->Outcomes
        ^          ^           | ^                    | |
        |          |_____| | |_____|  |
        |_____|                      |
        |_____|
```

speed of negotiation and the type, number, and quality of resultant outcomes (see Figure 2.5). That is, the greater the intensity of these factors,
the more rapidly the police organization attempts to neutralize or address the reaction of the community of concern.

SUMMARY

The process of public police violence can be conceptualized in terms
of four stages: media initiation, arousal, reaction, and outcomes. At any
point in the chain of events, the media or other actors can be aroused,
react, or produce an outcome (see Figure 2.5). Thus we have a cyclical—if
not an iterative—process whereby system and power maintenance is the
driving motivation of the police department (Koenig, 1985: 1). Norma-
tively, the less desirable outcomes are increased public relations efforts
and resistance; the most desirable outcomes are the new, practical, internal and external controls, implemented by or imposed upon the police.

The political process model is a general sketch of possibilities that can
unfold after an incident of public police violence. It is also a heuristic
tool that guides the collection of evidence and the way information from
different sources can be summarized. This model serves as a backdrop
for the development of a series of hypotheses to determine whether
arousal and reaction lead to increased control of police violence.

RESEARCH DESIGN AND METHODOLOGY

To empirically test as many hypotheses of this model as possible, ge-
ographic locations and cases and data to maximize the utility of the
model were chosen. This required a number of epistemological decisions
and compromises among countries, cities, and sources of data. In general, selected hypotheses of the model were tested in the context of reactions to public police violence in Toronto and New York City. Both
event data analysis and thick descriptive analysis were used. (See Appendix A for an in-depth discussion of research design and methodology.)

In terms of the two cultures, Canada generally promotes the interests of the community, while the United States stresses the rights of the individual (Lipset, 1968, 1985; Lipset and Pool, 1996). One might assume that Canadians would be more docile and less likely to protest against police misconduct than Americans. This, for example, would be an important reaction to police violence.

Events Database Analysis

Primary sources of data, such as police communication (e.g., officers' notes, informal talk, incident reports, radio logs) are not generally available to outsiders. But because the study is interested in outcomes, media accounts are probably the most important sources of information on "public" police violence.[11] Historically, the mass media, particularly newspapers, set a powerful agenda for change.

Consistent with the geographical and city focus of this study, the *New York Times Index* and *Canadian News Index* were used to access articles in the *New York Times* and *Toronto Star* and *Globe & Mail*, respectively. All items listed in these indexes dealing with police violence between January 1, 1977, and December 31, 1990, were listed and assembled into a master chronology.

Since most citations provide scant information on events of police violence, each article from microfilmed issues of the papers was photocopied. All of the pertinent information regarding each allegation was typed into a detailed chronology. Each case found was coded on a series of variables derived from the process model. (See Appendix B for the coding sheet.) The data was assembled into a Public Police Violence (PPV) data set. Appropriate statistical tests were performed on the data.

In-Depth Interviews

Semi-structured, face-to-face (and occasional telephone) interviews were conducted with people involved in and responding to many of the acts of police violence documented through the chronology and secondary source material (see Appendix C and Appendix D). In particular, three cases from each city (i.e., an act of police use of deadly force, police torture, and a police riot situation) generated the most media attention (measured in terms of numbers of newspaper citations) to form the final basis of analysis.

SUMMARY

What remains now is the analysis of the political process model in the context of each city: first Toronto and then New York City.

NOTES

1. This model is informed by a review of the academic literature, including, but not limited to, Sanders (1961), Cobb and Elder (1983), and Witte (1994), 55 semi-structured face-to-face interviews conducted with police officers, administrators, association and union officials, criminal lawyers, police reporters, broadcast journalists, editors, elected officials, and other members of the criminal justice system in Denver, Lethbridge, Montreal, New York City, and Toronto between 1989 and 1994. Research on reporters (i.e., Fishman, 1980: ch. 3) also suggests that they see a "typical event" as a series of phases. "The entire sequence of phases was [is] a phase structure portraying streams of interwoven activities as an object moving through a series of stages, or as a case moving through a career" (Fishman, 1980: 54–55).

2. For an in-depth discussion of this part of the model, see Ross (1998).

3. For a detailed description of this section, see Ross (1995a).

4. Many of the groups working to change the police, though not necessarily in the context of police violence, are outlined in Goldstein (1977: 311–328).

5. Also known as ignoring issues and apathy. It also may be boiled down to one of the tenets of organizational survival adopted by some employees: act surprised, act concerned, and admit to nothing.

6. This category subsumes Goldstein's (1977: 326) and includes protest, mobilization, and upheaval.

7. Admittedly, all reactions may be labeled public relations; separating cosmetic from deep-cutting ones requires a contextual analysis.

8. The first stage, evaluation, is transitional and of minimal cost. This includes the person or office who receives the news and how it is communicated throughout the bureaucracy. Decision is the choice among police alternatives or strategies, and implementation is putting those decisions into practice.

9. In April 1977, the 22-man New Paltz, New York police force was suspended by town officials after the American Home Assurance Company canceled its policy, citing 10 claims against the city for a total of 1.5 million (*New York Times*, April 3, 1977, Section I, p. 25).

10. Many of these actions are coterminous.

11. Outcomes are hard to observe and measure, because current negotiations are always influenced by the objective and subjective history of events and interactions. Perhaps the most common outcome is that media attention subsides when the news manufacturing process moves on to other issues. Interactive patterns of police-community violence continue whether or not an event is currently in the public eye.

Chapter 3

The Politics and Control of Police Violence in Toronto

There is a spit that runs along the eastern side of Toronto harbor. This land mass and the nearby islands minimize the winds and waves of Lake Ontario and naturally protect the waterfront. Originally created by years of silt and sand deposits from the Don River and erosion from the Scarborough bluffs, the spit has subsequently been built up with landfill from one or another public works and private development projects. During the day, the spit serves as home to Toronto's less desirable industries: oil refineries and junkyards line each side of Cherry Street, the road running the length of the spit. But at night, the land mass, particularly the park at the very end, serves another purpose: it is where some Toronto policemen occasionally bring people they "don't like," or those who give them "a hard time," and they beat them up. Isolated places like this are the domain of police forces across Canada and in most cities throughout the world. These clandestine locations are far removed from witnesses, allowing police to engage in back-alley justice. But Canadians like to think that they are different, in particular, more civilized than their neighbors to the south (see, e.g., Friedenberg, 1979; Lipset, 1968, 1985). Canadian history, however, particularly the myth of the peaceable kingdom, reveals less than benevolent police forces (Brown and Brown, 1978; Ross, 1995c, 1995d).

HISTORY OF REACTIONS TO POLICE VIOLENCE IN TORONTO

Besides having the largest municipal police force in Canada, Toronto has both the highest population and incidence of crime measured through either official or victimization statistics.[1] The police force was originally incorporated in 1834, roughly at the same time as the New York Police Department. It was during this time that the force developed its distinctly Orangeist organizational culture (i.e., ideological Toryism), the result of partisan appointments (who were Orangeist in nature) to the police force, which depended on city council nominations. Predictably, much of the latter part of the century was dominated by an effort by reform coalitions to stem the power of Orangeism in the department (Betcherman, 1982; Rogers, 1984).

At that time, the police force was dominated by Anglo-Saxon Protestants, most of them from Scotland and Northern Ireland. They made good police officers in the days when rawboned treatment of the criminal was judged the best way to law and order. To get ahead on the force, you had to be either a Mason or a member of the Orange Order, preferably both. In that respect, the police department wasn't any different from other civic departments. You needed some kind of political connection even to be considered for a civil service job. Wages of policemen and firemen were very good, and there was a pension too, something rare in industry in those days. (Thomas, 1991: 35)[2]

Several notable incidents of police violence took place after the force's incorporation, some of which inspired calls for increased controls. Historically speaking, there were eight often interrelated typical reactions to police violence in Toronto.

1. *Elected representatives supported police violence.* For example, between 1929 and 1930, Mayor Samuel McBride "publicly supported [Police Chief Brigadier-General Dennis C.] Draper's suppression of Red [communist] agitators" (Betcherman, 1982: 64). "Meanwhile, . . . Draper announced that he had investigated complaints of citizens allegedly manhandled by his men and found nothing in them. He branded as false the *Star's* reports of police brutality" (p. 65). On August 18, 1930, an inquiry chaired by Judge Emerson Coatsworth and labeled a "one, sided, slap-dash affair," concluded "that reports of rough usage were 'grossly exaggerated and in the major unworthy of any consideration or belief' " (p. 65).

2. *The media was often critical of police brutality.* During the fall of 1974, for example, the *Globe & Mail* published a series of articles on alleged Metro police brutality. To buttress the validity of the report, the *Globe* hired a respected lie detector technician, and 30 to 40 people claiming to have been abused by the police were tested. Subsequently, the paper ran approximately 13 of their stories. This prompted the Provincial Progressive Conservative (PC) government on October 23 of that year to authorize its own Royal Commission. Supervised by Justice Donald Morand, the findings, released almost two years later on June 30, 1976, made a series of recommendations, the most important of which con-

cerned the establishment of an independent police complaints investigation process (Ontario, 1976).

3. *Police officers were charged*. Several notable incidents of police violence took place after the force was amalgamated (incorporating the boroughs of North York, Scarborough, East York, Etobicoke, and the City of Toronto) on January 1, 1957. In 1958, it was discovered that three suspects, after being tortured, confessed to a series of gas station robberies they never committed (Thomas, 1991: 168). Three detectives from the Etobicoke police station, where the violent incident allegedly took place, were subsequently charged under the *Ontario Police Act*. The Metro Police Commission launched an investigation, and a Royal Commission was ordered. Shortly after the Royal Commission began, James F. Mackey, who at the time was a district commander, handled the investigation. According to Mackey, "There was no action taken against the police. Although some force had been used where these young men were concerned, they themselves were not without fault" (Mackey, 1985: 100). Chief John Chisholm (the new chief) "was visibly rocked by the scandal," and he suffered a major bout of depression, which finally led to suicide. Police violence was not prevalent in public discourse again until the early 1960s, when a series of raids on motorcycle gangs provoked cries of police brutality (Mackey, 1985: 132).

4. *The public supported violence by the Metro Toronto Police Force (MTPF)*. Since the early 1960s, Toronto has become more culturally and ethnically diverse. There has been a large influx of immigrants, including visible minorities from the Caribbean and Asia. This has created an increased number of conflicts involving the police. Fear that Toronto would experience the televised level of crime and urban disorder that permeated the United States during the 1960s—combined with good old-fashioned British xenophobia—compelled the police to target drug and morality related crimes. Homophobia also permeated certain levels of the police department. In contrast to American police forces, police corruption was virtually unheard of in Canadian police departments. This situation encouraged public trust of the police among white, middle-class Torontonians.[3] Torontonians also compared themselves to Montréalers, and the MTPF prided themselves in not letting the city fall prey to the high incidence of bank robberies that Montréal experienced during this time period.[4] Further, certain MTPF squads and officers either felt like or were authorized to be "the prince of the city" and were provided carte blanche status by senior administration in their investigations.[5] It also led to a so-called "punishment syndrome," where officers felt that they could use excessive psychological and physical violence against those suspected of having committed crimes.

5. *The mass media were occasionally sympathetic toward police use of violence*. For example, on October 3, 1871, during a riot of young Britons,

the police "intervened to prevent the destruction of Cosgrove's tavern, the major rendezvous for Toronto Fenians. Although the *Leader* believed the force used its pistols too freely in these disturbances and shot indiscriminately at fleeing spectators, most newspapers commended the police for their restraint" (Rogers, 1984: 131).

During the depression, Chief Draper, "nudged by his business friends" (Thomas, 1991: 36), ordered officers to harass communists and break up their meetings and demonstrations.

Under his regime law enforcement was Draconian. . . . His admiration for American police methods included their handling of Red Agitators. . . . Draper started his offensive against local Communists . . . by setting up a Red Squad composed of three policemen notorious for their strong-arm tactics. (Betcherman, 1982: 15)

In 1929 and 1930, a series of peaceful gatherings on street corners by soap-box orators and protest meetings at Queen's Park, where the Ontario legislature is located, led to a number of violent police actions by Draper's "Dragoons" against communists and innocent bystanders (Betcherman, 1982; Thomas, 1991: 36). Although the *Star* was highly critical of the police, and there were several calls for inquiries by various groups, including organized labor (Betcherman, 1982: 64), the *Globe* and *Mail and Empire*[6] were generally supportive of police actions.

6. *Commissions of inquiry were ordered.* The first recorded incidents of police violence occurred when constables broke up reformist political meetings after the Rebellion of 1837 and the general election of 1841. The latter prompted a provincial inquiry: "The police were rounded up and condemned for their partiality" (Rogers, 1984: 118). Furthermore, in 1849, "the police were implicated in the violent public protests over William Lyon Mackenzie's return to Toronto" and "the Rebellion Losses Bill" (p. 119). "A public inquiry was called for but city council avoided the issue" (ibid.).

Over a century later, on October 24, 1971, during a visit by Soviet Premier Alexi Kosygin to the Ontario Science Centre, there was a violent confrontation between demonstrators and MTPF officers. Thirteen members of the public were injured, and five police were hurt after mounted police charged into the crowd.[7] Consequently, on October 25, 1971, a Royal Commission, under the chairmanship of Judge Ilvio Anthony Vannini, was ordered by the Ontario government[8] to investigate the disturbance. The report, completed on June 5, 1972, suggested that police were overzealous in their actions. Specifically, it outlined incidents of police abuse where excessive and brutal force was used while officers were effecting their arrests. It also made recommendations regarding police behavior in demonstration situations (Ontario, 1972).

And on April 19, 1974, several letters were tabled before the Metro

Council Executive Committee from residents of Rochdale College, an alternative and a highly controversial institution of higher learning, who were complaining of physical abuse and harassment by police. As a result, the Committee asked the Metropolitan Toronto Police Board to draft a report. Almost a month later, on May 16, the board publicly sanctioned a proposal for a review of operations of the Metro Police complaint procedures. The Board of Police Commissioners approved the proposal. The inquiry, conducted by respected criminal lawyer Arthur Maloney, was designed to determine whether proper complaint procedures were being followed by the police. There was no official mandate, however, to find out whether abuses were in fact occurring.

Among the various findings of the Maloney Report (publicly released a year later, on May 12, 1975, during Canadian Police Week) were that police commonly cover up when a fellow officer is accused in a complaint, and that the existing complaints procedure, totally under the administrative control of the Force, was often another form of whitewash. The most important recommendation of the Report was the appointment of an independent Commissioner of Citizen Complaints to be appointed by the Metro (Toronto) Council (Maloney, 1975). These recommendations were finally implemented six years later, in 1981.

7. *The police department periodically used public relations to counteract public criticism.* Negative attention was partly minimized through the "Public and Community Relations Bureau," established in July 1961. According to that year's Annual Report, which was widely disseminated, the Bureau was constituted to "coordinate policemen who were made available to citizen groups, the press, radio and television stations for purposes of discussing problems peculiar to policing" (Metropolitan Toronto, Board of Commissioners of Police, *Annual Report*, 1960: 14). In 1963, the stated purpose of this Bureau changed: the main function of the unit was to facilitate "a better understanding between the citizens of the community and the members of the Metro Toronto Police." The program of the Bureau was designed to "stress the need for such mutual interdependence in containing the growth of crime and traffic accidents" (Metropolitan Toronto Board of Commissioners of Police, *Annual Report*, 1963: 17). Even though in 1963 the stress was on the word "community," the Annual Reports of the following years emphasized the importance of entertainment activities such as the Male Chorus, Pipe Bandstand, and Mounted Unit Musical Ride as important aspects of this department.

In 1967, the MTPF appointed two officers to work as Community Service Officers (CSOs) in the Regent Park government housing project. According to that year's Annual Report, they patrolled the area from 7:00 P.M. to 3:00 A.M., the periods during which most property damage occurred, and claimed to have established credibility with individual tenants, the Tenants' Association, various social service agencies, and other segments of the community. According to police reports, the incidence of crime decreased as a result of this intervention.

In 1969, CSOs were assigned to the Yorkville and Alexander Park areas. The CSO program officially came into operation in May 1970, when 22 police officers were assigned to the project. After receiving training from psychiatrists, psychologists, social workers, and family counseling services, the officers returned to their respective divisions. Over time they found themselves working with drop-in centers and youth organizations, setting up recreational activities and generally opening up lines of communication with agencies and groups operating within their jurisdiction. The program still exists today under the Community Program Division of the MTPF. In 1973, the Police Ethnic Relations Unit (PERU) was created to work in the ethnic communities and to cope with the changing needs of the city's different ethnic groups. When the unit was established, it was composed of nine police officers from diverse ethnic backgrounds (Dunlop and Greenway, 1972; Metropolitan Toronto Board of Commissioners of Police, *Annual Report*, 1983). Although the police maintain that the program is a success, there has been no independent evaluation to date.

8. *Finally, elements of the public protested against real or alleged police violence*. At the turn of the century, "there was a growing public dislike of the use of violence by the force against supposed felons and any other individuals who were believed to be enemies of the force, or of their political patrons on the city council" (Jarvis, 1979: 74). On the other hand, "[f]ew men were ever dismissed for cause from service during the 1860s. This fact could indicate that all the detailed regulations were followed more often than not—it could also mean, however, that they were not followed at all" (Jarvis, 1979: 79).

On May 4, 1969, Angelo Nobrega was shot by plainclothes detectives: "[A]ccording to police reports Angelo refused to stop when instructed by police officers." The police chased Nobrega's car, shot him, and he later died. "Police officials described the shooting as accidental" (Bourne and Eisenberg, 1972: 12). After the Nobrega shooting, however, "a number of events occurred that caused widespread attention to be focused on this incident. First, on May 5, a church rally protesting the shooting took place, and it was attended by 80 members of Toronto's Portuguese community. This was followed a week later by a front-page editorial in the *Corrio Portuguese*, a weekly newspaper for the Portuguese people of Toronto. . . . Two days after this editorial appeared, 500 members of Toronto's Portuguese community marched silently through the city's downtown streets to protest the shooting" (Bourne and Eisenberg, 1972: 12–13). An inquest followed, and the jury determined that the shooting was accidental, exonerated Detective Boyd, and recommended that members of the public be more cooperative with the police. Although this should have ended the case, some local newspaper editorials criticized both the coroner's charge to the jury and the verdict handed down by them. (p. 22)

Another controversial example of brutality that led to public protest occurred on February 5, 1981, when four gay bathhouses were simultaneously raided by over 200 police officers.[9] This led to a major outcry by those charged, other members of the homosexual community, and civil libertarians. This outrage was further buttressed when undercover police were accused of being agent provocateurs in the subsequent march to protest the raids. Once again, the incident resulted in a commissioned report that offered a variety of recommendations (see, e.g., Bruner, 1981).

A feeble attempt to restrain the police was made in June 1980, with Provincial Bill 47 (the *Metropolitan Police Force Complaints Project Act*). Unfortunately, due to legal flaws, it was not even reviewed by a committee of the legislature. Two months after the 1981 provincial election (May 1981), Bill 47, redrafted as Bill 68, was tabled by the provincial government. Subsequently, a coalition against the legislation, representing over 40 community and ethnic groups, protested under the slogan: "Wanted: A just and independent police complaints procedure 1981."

During the 1980s, members of the Jane-Finch and Regent Park communities (the first is an area where a large concentration of blacks live, and the latter is Canada's largest public housing project) complained of entrapment and police harassment. This effected the formation of groups such as the Regent Park Committee Against Police Harassment. Other incidents of police misconduct (e.g., the Neil Proverbs and Charles Keeping incidents) subjected the force to increased public scrutiny in the middle of the decade.

Between the summer of 1988 and spring of 1990, there were three shootings of blacks in Toronto and two just outside of the city. These events led to increased animosity between the police and the black community. In Toronto, Lester Donaldson, age 43, partially crippled, but allegedly brandishing a knife, was killed on August 9, 1988, when four policemen responded to a call and shot him in his kitchen. On October 27, 1989, Sophia Cook, also black, was a passenger in a reportedly stolen car stopped by police officers. During "an altercation" between one of the police and the two men in the car, the officer's gun was fired. The bullet hit her spine and paralyzed her from the waist down. And on May 14, 1990, Marlon Neal, 16, was shot in the back by two of the three bullets fired by Metro policemen at a radar trap, and he subsequently died. These incidents contributed to a well-publicized case of "blaming the victim," especially when Alan Tonks and June Rolands of the Police Commission suggested that it was logical for the police to fear blacks because they commit a disproportionate amount of crime. Furthermore, Tonks also told a legislative committee that police *were* treating blacks differently. Although he later apologized for these comments, such statements merely reinforced police biases, increased paranoia among citizens, and infuriated law-abiding, visible minorities. In an effort to appease the public, the New Democratic Party-led Ontario government established the "Ontario Race Relations and Policing Inquiry" in 1989, which led to a revision of the *Police Act* of Ontario into what is now called the *Police Services Act*. Opposition critics complained that the provincial liberals were reforming the *Police Act* anyway and simply put other issues on hold to pass the new legislation. Many of these actions stimulated calls, if not changes, in the control of the police. The bathhouse raids, complaints by visible minorities, and police demonstration control efforts have all been subjects of complaints during the last three decades. For almost all of them, reports were written. Yet controls in Toronto are unique enough to merit discussion.

CONTROLLING THE MTPF[10]

The type of controls on the MTPF are similar to those generally found in most big-city police departments throughout North America. Following earlier distinctions, controls on the MTPF can be divided generally into internal and external mechanisms.

Internal Mechanisms

Eight major forms of formal internal controls that operate in the MTPF are commissioned reports, standing orders and *Rules and Regulations*, shooting requalifications, Internal Affairs, hiring requirements and training procedures, trials office, the *Police Act* (now replaced by the *Police Services Act*), and the Chief of Police.[11]

External Mechanisms

External mechanisms of control can be loosely divided into governmental and public processes. The degree of control over the MTPF by external governmental authorities is complicated and varies with different levels of government. In general, the onus of control is placed in the hands of the provincial legislature, with the municipality serving a symbolic role. Governmental external controls are, in increasing order of importance: the Ontario Human Rights Commission, the Ontario Police Commission, the Ontario Solicitor General's office, the Metro Council, the Board of Commissioners, and the Office of the Public Complaints Commissioner (OPCC).[12]

Several public external mechanisms also exist. They are, in increasing order of importance: ad hoc groups, the Canadian Civil Liberties Association (CCLA), the Metropolitan Toronto Police Association (MTPA), the media, and public opinion. It should be mentioned, however, that police public relations efforts serve as a veritable impediment to change.

RESULTS FROM EPISODE CHARACTERISTICS, REACTION, AND OUTCOME VARIABLES

History, controls, and perceptions of police violence aside, what is the empirical evidence of police violence between 1977 and 1990? This is difficult to ascertain, as comprehensive data on police violence in Toronto does not exist (Ross, 1995d). However, the data of two organizations (CIRPA and OPCC) was compared to that generated by this study. Clearly, the number of events reported in CIRPA's and OPCC's data far surpasses those captured in this study's data set, ranging from a 3:1 to a 52:1 ratio, respectively. From 1977 to 1990, there were a total of 51 public police violence events (see Table 3.1).

Twenty-three attributes, including single and/or combinations of variables from the public police violence (PPV) data set, are explored in this section. The first 10, collectively called episode characteristics, refer to the timing, type, perpetrators, and targets of the attacks. The next nine refer to reactions by the public, government, and police. Finally, the remaining four refer to control outcomes. Likewise, all of the variables have measurement difficulties, however, these will not be discussed here. Although some of the variables have considerable missing data, I believe that the results confirm most of the options that individuals and organizations take as articulated in the political process model.

Episode Characteristics[13]

Unlike New York City, Toronto has consistently experienced a low annual level of public police violence (see Table 3.1). No major trend is apparent from visual inspection of the table; the number of incidents remains somewhat constant with the exception of two peaks in 1980 and 1984. Coterminously, almost 50 percent of the events took place during the first five years of the data, before the Jack Marks and William McCormick administrations. It is interesting to note that after these peaks and five-year period, there was a constant decrease in the number of recorded acts of police violence. In fact, the two peaks are separated by a three-year period, but no other crest is apparent, and no major increase is noted from 1984 onward. Perhaps this suggests that after several pub-

Table 3.1

Comparison of Complaints of Police Violence Based on Different Organizations and Their Classifications

Year	CIRPA[a]	OPCC[b]	Public Police Violence
1977			4
1978			2
1979			5
1980			6
1981			5
1982	52	290	4
1983	43	385	4
1984	48	302	6
1985		385	1
1986		347	1
1987		386	3
1988		303	3
1989		297	3
1990			3
Missing			1
	-----	-----	-----
TOTAL	143		51

a. Based on actions classified as violence.
b. Based on actions classified as Assault and Physical Assault/Excessive Force, listed in the tables "Types of Complaint Allegations Filed" and "Type of Allegation" from the organization's annual reports, 1982–1989. These incidents include such actions as assault, common assault, assault causing bodily harm, assault with injury, assault while restrained, and sexual assault. (In 1990, the OPCC was subsumed by the Ontario Public Complaints Commission.)

licized incidents of police violence, this kind of police behavior is more at bay and more "controlled." This may reflect public outcry, the deterrent effect of the OPCC, and/or the police's perception of public condemnation, including the ability of Chiefs Marks and McCormick to influence their ranks to curtail violent acts more successfully than did their predecessors. Nevertheless, annual trends are merely rough consolidations of more intricate patterns.

The bulk of allegations of police violence consists of unspecified police brutality (41%); the second-place positions go to beatings and unspecified killings (26% and 18%, respectively); and there was a minimal number of cases (6%) involving some type of torture (see Table 3.2).

Since the age differences between the police officer(s) and the victim(s) and the weight of the victim (s) and police officer (s) were missing from most cases, they were excluded from this analysis. Looking at the status of the victim, we find that in 88 percent of cases, the person who was allegedly abused by the police was most likely an average citizen, not a public figure (see Table 3.3).

Of the cases that could be identified, the majority of victims were male (84%) interacting mainly with male police officers (71%) (see Table 3.4).

Table 3.2
Severity (Degree of Harm to Victim)

	Frequency	Percent
Torture	3	5.9
Deadly Force (may or may not result in death)	5	9.8
Killing (unspecified)	9	17.6
Beating (includes assault)	13	25.5
Brutality (unspecified/misc.)	21	41.2
	-----	-----
TOTAL	51	100.0

Table 3.3
Status of Victim[a]

	Frequency	Percent
Yes	5	9.8
No	45	88.2
Missing	1	2.0
	-----	-----
TOTAL	51	100.0

a. Whether or not victim was a public figure.

Table 3.4
Gender of Participant/s

	Victims		Police Officers	
	Frequency	Percent	Frequency	Percent
Female	3	5.9	0	
Male	43	84.3	36	70.6
Missing	5	9.8	15	29.4
	-----	-----	-----	-----
TOTAL	51	100.0	51	100.0

Of those incidents coded, 24 percent of the victims were visible minorities. Caucasian victims comprised 16 percent of the sample (see Table 3.5). The reverse was true of police officers; 26 percent were Caucasian. Although this information was missing for the majority of cases, the force, during this time period, was composed mostly of white officers. Thus, on a random basis, the police officer involved would almost always be white. Roughly 69 percent of the incidents led to a criminal charge being laid against the police officer (see Table 3.6), which most likely contributed to the public's perception of police officers' wrongdoing. Although a lack of conviction for the officer may provoke a convinced public to cry foul, a guilty verdict satisfies the converts and changes the opinions of those who doubted the criminal behavior of the officer in question.

Table 3.5
Race of Participants in Police Violence

| | Victims | | Police Officers | |
	Frequency	Percent	Frequency	Percent
White	8	15.7	13	25.5
Visible minority	12	23.5		
Missing	31	60.8	38	74.5
TOTAL	51	100.0	51	100.0

Table 3.6
Perception of Illegality of Case

	Frequency	Percent
Criminal charge against officer(s) was discussed	35	68.6
Undetermined	16	31.4
TOTAL	51	100.0

Table 3.7
Number of Participants

| No. | Victims | | No. | Police Officers | |
	Frequency	Percent		Frequency	Percent
1	44	86.3	1	14	27.5
2	1	2.0	2	17	33.3
3	1	2.0	3	1	2.0
			4	2	3.9
			5	1	2.0
			7	1	2.0
Missing	5	9.8		15	29.4
TOTAL	51	100.0		51	100.0

Percentages do not equal 100 due to rounding.

The majority of cases (86%) had one victim; only 2 percent had two and three each (see Table 3.7). This relatively small number of victims may have contributed to the public's perception that the problem of police violence was not prevalent, thus dulling their reaction. Also, almost half of the incidents involved only one officer, and about 40 percent included two; the rest had from two to seven officers participating.

There was a greater range in the ages of the victims than in the police officers' ages, which were mostly missing. Although 6 percent of the victims were 19 years old, no other pattern was discerned (see Table 3.8).

It might be futile to comment on the demeanor of the victims, since most information regarding their physical or mental demeanor was missing (see Table 3.9). However, this factor in itself may be interesting. Ei-

Table 3.8
Age of Participants

Age	Victims Frequency	Victims Percent	Police Officers Frequency	Police Officers Percent
16	1	2.0		
19	3	5.9		
23	1	2.0		
24	1	2.0	1	2.0
25	1	2.0		
27	1	2.0	1	2.0
30	1	2.0		
35	1	2.0	1	2.0
38	1	2.0		
44	1	2.0	1	2.0
48	1	2.0		
52	1	2.0		
Missing	37	72.5	47	92.0
TOTAL	51	100.0	51	100.0

Percentages do not equal 100 due to rounding.

Table 3.9
Demeanor of Subject

	Frequency	Percent
Mentally ill	1	2.0
Intoxicated	5	9.8
Missing	45	88.2
TOTAL	51	100.0

Table 3.10
Activity Level of Victim

	Frequency	Percent
Victim was active[a]	9	17.6
Victim carried weapon[b]	6	11.8
Victim was passive[c]	18	35.3
Missing	18	35.3
TOTAL	51	100.0

a. Put up resistance.
b. Includes fake.
c. Includes handcuffed and running away.

ther all of the victims were sober and only a small percentage of them (12%) were either intoxicated or mentally ill, or this is an item journalists do not investigate, or editorial decisions have been made to exclude it. Furthermore, of those cases coded for victim's behavior, 35 percent of them were passive, offering no resistance to arrest (see Table 3.10); 18

Table 3.11
Number of Articles that the Incident Generated

No. of Articles	Frequency	Percent
9	1	2.0
10	1	2.0
13	1	2.0
14	1	2.0
22	1	2.0
28	1	2.0
37	1	2.0
12	2	3.9
16	2	3.9
7	2	3.9
5	2	3.9
4	4	7.8
3	5	9.8
2	6	11.8
1	21	41.2
TOTAL	51	100.0

Percentages do not equal 100 due to rounding.

percent were active and only 12 percent carried weapons. Based on this alone, one might argue that only 12 percent of the cases required police to be more "forceful."

Reaction Variables[14]

Almost 41 percent of the incidents were mentioned in only one newspaper article. The rest of the events generated from 10 to 37 articles. This implies that almost half of the cases involving police violence may go unnoticed by the public (see Table 3.11). In terms of the number of citations, the incidents of police violence that garnered a considerable amount of media attention and loosely correspond with the largest number of *Globe & Mail* and *Toronto Star* newspaper index citations were investigated, including the shooting of Buddy Evans (28) (August 9, 1978), the torture of Rodney Turner (9) (May 15, 1979), and the Morrish Road police riot incident (3) (May 29, 1982).[15]

Similarly, 40 percent of the cases received no follow-up, as inferred from the time lapsed between the first and last articles (see Table 3.12). This lack of exposure contributes to the collective amnesia of the community. It is difficult to become concerned about police abuse if cases are sporadically reported, are not connected to one another or to similar incidents, or are printed or broadcast only once. This process may also transpire even when events are followed up after a considerable amount of time has lapsed since they first occurred. In other words, these inci-

Table 3.12
Days Elapsed between First and Last Article on Incident

Days	Frequency	Percent
0	20	39.2
2	1	2.0
9	1	2.0
12	1	2.0
19	1	2.0
42	1	2.0
46	1	2.0
48	1	2.0
53	1	2.0
86	1	2.0
111	1	2.0
150	1	2.0
192	1	2.0
201	1	2.0
209	1	2.0
234	1	2.0
275	1	2.0
280	1	2.0
311	1	2.0
450	1	2.0
477	1	2.0
487	1	2.0
520	1	2.0
548	1	2.0
692	1	2.0
732	1	2.0
773	1	2.0
832	1	2.0
855	1	2.0
981	1	2.0
1,276	1	2.0
3,087	1	2.0
TOTAL	51	100.0

Percentages do not equal 100 due to rounding.

dents may then be more difficult to react to as they may have faded from peoples' memories. With the passage of time, anger and other salient emotions and memories fade. Thus, it is difficult to reopen old wounds, particularly when they were not that deep to begin with.

Another way of conceptualizing reaction is scope, or the number of actors that get involved beyond the victims, police officers, and department. This variable consists of all of those people interviewed for the newspaper articles who are representatives of organizations. About 35 percent of cases had only one such actor involved. Ten was the highest number of people involved, but this occurred in only one of the cases (see Table 3.13). The scope of the incidents is thus relatively small.

Public organization reactions are generally low. Only 10 percent of the cases precipitated some kind of public demonstration, while interest

Table 3.13
Scope[a]

No. of People	Frequency	Percent
1	18	35.3
2	12	23.5
3	6	11.8
4	3	5.9
5	3	5.9
6	1	2.0
7	2	3.9
9	1	2.0
10	1	2.0
Missing	4	7.8
TOTAL	51	100.0

a. Scope refers to the number of actors who got involved in the incident after it took place. Percentages do not equal 100 due to rounding.

Table 3.14
Citizens Group/Organizations Reactions

	Frequency	Percent
Former president of police association complains	2	3.9
Citizens (non victims) complain	2	3.9
Interest groups call for public inquiry	3	5.9
Interest groups complain	3	5.9
Public demonstration	5	9.8
Missing	36	70.6
TOTAL	51	100.0

group involvement was as low as 6 percent (see Table 3.14). Again, this must be interpreted with caution, since most information was missing, making firm conclusions on the above data inappropriate.

The media reaction to these types of events is generally weak; in only 2 percent of cases did the journalist criticize the police for not following procedures and wrote about supporting interest groups in only 6 percent (see Table 3.15). The most common reaction for victims is to launch a complaint (12%); for government agencies (i.e., courts, justices, juries), it is to acquit the officer of wrongdoing (16%); and for the accused officers, it is to suppress the facts or provide information on wrongdoing (12%) (see Tables 3.16, 3.17, 3.18, respectively). It is noteworthy that police officers regularly use this type of deception (i.e., covering up their acts) in responding to their charges. This is particularly interesting considering that the government's main response is to acquit their officers. Although

Table 3.15
Media Reaction

	Frequency	Percent
Mentions elements of attack are broadcast on television	1	2.0
Columnist says procedures are not being followed	1	2.0
Columnist writes critique of event	3	5.9
Missing	46	90.2
	-----	-----
TOTAL	51	100.0

Percentages do not equal 100 due to rounding.

Table 3.16
Victims' and Victims' Relatives' Reaction

	Frequency	Percent
Hires lawyer	1	2.0
Sues police/launches civil action	2	3.9
Tells story to the newspaper	3	5.9
Lays charge against the police	3	5.9
Launches complaint with police complaints division	6	11.8
Launches complaint (misc.)	12	23.5
Missing	24	47.0
	-----	-----
TOTAL	51	100.0

Table 3.17
Government Agencies' Reaction

	Frequency	Percent
CCJJ[a] considers law to apply	1	2.0
CCJJ convicts officer of some charges	1	2.0
CCJJ upholds acquittal	1	2.0
Accused is exonerated	1	2.0
Complaint Board official criticizes slow procedure	1	2.0
CCJJ sentences officer(s)	2	3.9
Coroner gives decision	2	3.9
Attorney office probes allegations	3	5.9
CCJJ awards victim(s) financial compensation	3	5.9
CCJJ convicts officer(s)	4	7.8
CCJJ lays charge	6	11.8
CCJJ acquits officer(s)	8	15.7
Missing	18	35.3
	-----	-----
TOTAL	51	100.0

a. CCJJ is crown, courts, judge, or jury.
Percentages do not equal 100 due to rounding.

Table 3.18
Accused Officer's Reaction

	Frequency	Percent
Appeals court decision	1	2.0
Pleads guilty	1	2.0
Sues plaintiff (victims)	1	2.0
Misses inquest	2	3.9
Appeals departmental decisions	2	3.9
Says victim(s) threatened him or his family	4	7.8
Suppresses facts or provides false information surrounding case/refused questioning	6	11.8
Missing	34	66.7
TOTAL	51	100.0

Percentages do not equal 100 due to rounding.

Table 3.19
Elected Officials' Reactions

	Frequency	Percent
Opposition party leader calls for new investigation	1	2.0
Opposition party leader promises to push public inquiry	1	2.0
Party in power attempts to calm protest by positive comments about improvements in black/police relations	1	2.0
Opposition party says Solicitor General is violating the law	1	2.0
Missing	47	92.2
TOTAL	51	100.0

Percentages do not equal 100 due to rounding.

most of the information is missing, it is worth mentioning the lack of reaction displayed by most elected officials (see Table 3.19). There is a good probability that if these individuals initiated a response, it would have been reported in the newspapers. Thus it is safe to assume that, for the most part, they do nothing that would generate a media report.

The Control Outcomes

The most frequent internal control outcome against officers is to launch an internal affairs investigation (14%), while the next most common is

Table 3.20
Internal Control Outcomes Against Officer

	Frequency	Percent
Charges officer(s) with criminal offense	1	2.0
Suspends officer(s) from department	1	2.0
Dismisses/fires officer(s)	1	2.0
Suspended officer/s without pay	1	2.0
Officer placed on paid leave	1	2.0
Orders officer(s) work without pay	2	3.9
Reprimands officer(s)	2	3.9
Launches internal investigation	3	5.9
Internal Affairs investigates	7	13.7
Missing	32	62.7
TOTAL	51	100.0

Percentages do not equal 100 due to rounding.

Table 3.21
Internal Control Initiatives Against Entire Police Force

	Frequency	Percent
Implements new regulations	1	2.0
Requests judicial inquiry	1	2.0
Releases public report on events	1	2.0
Implements reforms	2	3.9
Missing	46	90.2
TOTAL	51	100.0

Percentages do not equal 100 due to rounding.

starting an internal investigation, followed by an order for officers to work without pay (see Table 3.20).

When the entire police force is affected through internal control initiatives, responses range from the implementation of reforms (4%) to releases of reports to the public (2%). The majority of cases are missing here, so this is a mere comment on what actually takes place (see Table 3.21).

Finally, the most common (12%) external control initiative is an inquest initiated by the government. The release of a report by the coroner's office (10%) is next; only 2 percent of the cases had a Police Commissioner launching an inquiry (see Table 3.22).

A factor that mitigates external control is the police department public relations and resistance to the complaints. The most common response

Table 3.22
External Control Initiatives Against Police Force

	Frequency	Percent
Solicitor General investigates	1	2.0
Police commission launches inquiry	1	2.0
Government asks third party to intervene	2	3.9
Grand jury investigates	2	3.9
Attorney General advises person to relay charge	2	3.9
Coroner releases report	5	9.8
Government initiates inquest	6	11.8
Missing	32	62.7
	-----	-----
TOTAL	51	100.0

Table 3.23
Police Department Public Relations and Resistance

	Frequency	Percent
Suspends investigation	1	2.0
Publishes figures on its ability to combat crime	1	2.0
Promises public apology and financial retribution	1	2.0
Police says victim resisted, was aggressive, or dangerous	1	2.0
Chief says department is capable of good investigation into incident	1	2.0
Chief says that victim will file lawsuit	1	2.0
Department claims normal procedures were respected	1	2.0
Rejects complaint	6	11.8
Missing	38	74.5
	-----	-----
TOTAL	51	100.0

Percentages do not equal 100 due to rounding.

(12%) by the police is to reject the complaint (see Table 3.23). If police efforts are successful, no further response is necessary by either internal or external bodies of control. This may indeed be the case, judging from the meager response by government officials.

SUMMARY

In general, the data point to the following picture: the average victim of police violence is black, the police officer is white, in 50 percent of the cases there is no follow-up story, and thus, based on the media report, we do not have a comprehensive picture of how the police department and other relevant actors respond. The major shortcomings of this type of data can be remedied, in part, by considering the following three case studies of police violence in Toronto. The shooting of Andrew (Buddy) Evans, the alleged torture of Rodney Edward Turner, and the Morrish Road police riot reveal more subtle patterns evident in the process of public police violence.

INTENSIVE CASE STUDIES

Deadly Force: Andrew (Buddy) Evans (August 9, 1978)[16]

Andrew (Buddy) Evans, 24, a black man, was shot to death by Metro Toronto police constable John Clark, also 24, in front of the now-defunct downtown Flying Disco Tavern on King Street West. Buddy went to the bar to defend "the honor" of Peter Preston, his younger brother, who had an argument with the bouncer concerning a waitress. Preston apparently also had a machete hidden in a garbage bag. Clark, a rookie policeman, responded to the call. According to police, Evans attacked Clark with the man's own billy club and was shot by the policeman from a 10 to 15 feet distance. Buddy was "a big guy, almost scary, and could have been just waving his hand," a friend of the victim, interviewed by me, suggested. Buddy was from "down east," (i.e., Nova Scotia). His mother was a school teacher and made sure the boys had a good education, but he was no angel. Buddy claimed that he was harassed by the police, especially when driving a cab in Toronto, and that the Halifax Police Department warned the MTPF about him. He had also done time for petty crimes.[17]

Media Initiation

The media was quick to respond. The story made good copy in a city that was already experiencing a number of highly publicized incidents of racism against the increasing black population. But the Evans situation was different. It was not against a newly arrived emigrant from Jamaica, fleeing social and political unrest; it was directed against a Canadian citizen from the Maritimes. According to Mal Connoly, former director of the MTPA, "The police reacted with outrage at the fact that he (Clark) was convicted by the media and the citizenry. The media treated it wrong. The media kept on going to [Charlie] Roach, [Dudley] Laws, and [Jack] Pinkovsky [activist criminal defense lawyers that were media savvy]. Eventually I got a call from Christie Blatchford, when she was with the *Toronto Star*," a fair reporter. Connoly complained that the media never contacted him, but pandered to the activists.[18] In reality, though, the media did very little reporting until a little over a year later, when the inquest began. The newspaper reports were sustained by the same reporters, Arthur Johnson and Ross Laver, in both of the daily major newspapers at that time.

Arousal

Just after Evans was shot, a number of other police officers arrived on the scene. They took the rookie, who had fainted, to the hospital, while Evans was left bleeding inside of the restaurant. Some witnesses say that the police let Evans bleed to death, and that quick action on the police's part would have saved him. Besides the victim, the incident also involved Buddy's brother, the black community, the coroner, the "tough on police" mayor (John Sewell at the time), the police force, and the victim's family's and police officer's respective lawyers. It eventually involved vocal members of organizations in the black community and the MTPA.

Reaction

Preston was arrested and charged with possession of a dangerous weapon, a machete. The shooting sparked strong protests from some members of the black community and accusations that police had killed Evans without justification. Within hours of the shooting, there was an official police version that the shooting was done in self-defense, and an unofficial explanation among the black community that it was an unjustified racial killing. The night of the incident, about 40 demonstrators marched to City Hall to protest the killing. While some protesters accused police of murder and paraded outside of City Hall chanting, "We want justice," other members of the community had mobilized support that manifested itself in letters to the editor and high-level contacts with the police department.[19]

The family originally hired Charles Roach to represent them at the inquest, which began on May 14 and ended on November 30, 1979, almost a year after the shooting, but according to him, the family disagreed with his approach to the case. There was some difference of opinion over having the case go before the coroner. Roach clarified, "[T]hey had different ways of solving the case. Thus we separated. I do not separate my role of lawyer in the courts from a lawyer who wants to change the police. I spent time getting people down to the coroners' office." Jack Pinkofsky, Roach's former Osgood Hall classmate, took over the case, while Roach and Laws engaged in political work connected to the inquest. When all was said and done, Dave Martin, Pinkofsky's partner, did most of the work on the matter. Later, when Pinkofsky suffered a heart attack, Roach ended up completing the case.[20]

The shooting was investigated at an inquest beginning on October 10, with Coroner Peter King originally in attendance. Austin Cooper, representing Clark, like the police department, framed the incident in terms of self-defense. In this view, Clark was protecting his life when he shot Evans. Pinkofsky, representing the Evans family, portrayed the incident as a racial attack. The inquest was halted several times. Coroner Margaret Milton, who eventually took over the inquiry, stopped the proceedings, for example, after antagonisms that were building erupted into a shouting match between Pinkofsky and Cooper.

During the inquest, a number of significant facts were uncovered. One of them damaged the Evans case, while the others muted police reactions. First, just one night before the incident, Evans had threatened to "blow away" the tavern's bouncer. Constable Dennis Orchard testified that bouncer Franklyn Bramble told him that Evans had made the threat because Preston was asked to leave the bar a week earlier. Orchard said that he was called to the bar earlier that night because Bramble feared that Evans would attack him. Additionally, testimony indicated that Clark fired after Evans struck him on the head and near the groin with a billy club that he had grabbed from Clark. However, it was discovered that Evans had dropped the club he was brandishing and that he had his hands in a surrendering gesture when he was shot by Clark. After the inquest, Clark was not charged with any wrongdoing.[21]

Second, the Ontario government's Committee on Race Relations was established during this time with Roy McMurtry, a prominent Toronto attorney as chair. It was created to help the MTPF deal with a large influx of black and Asian immigrants to Toronto. This committee recommended that similar bodies be set up at the municipal level throughout the province. This program was in conjunction with Law Enforcement-Race Relations Committees that were established in 1977 in the Jane-Finch, Regent Park, and Parkdale areas; a fourth committee was established in Rexdale in May 1978. These organizations were created to facilitate communication between police officials and members of visible minority groups, as well as to enable members of visible minorities to better understand methods and procedures associated with effective policing. Unfortunately, these committees were largely ineffective (Gandy, 1979; Stasiulis, 1989). Understandably, due to organizational restructuring, they have since been phased out.

Simultaneously, in 1977, the Police Ethnic Relations Unit (PERU) expanded through the inclusion of a "Black and East Indian division." During the summer of 1980, PERU consisted of 15 men out of a force comprised, at that time, of 5,400 members. The types of incidents the unit was called upon to mediate included noise complaints, name-calling leading to assault, assault causing bodily harm, and violence in schools. The unit did not have a mandate to resolve disputes involving alleged police mistreatment of minorities or racism in the police force. According to Stasiulis (1989: 70),

PERU has had limited impact on the nature of policing in the city, by virtue of its small size, the junior rank of its officers, and its isolation from the everyday, run-of-the-mill police duties engaged in by the majority of the force. The unit has been successful, however, in projecting a positive image to counterbalance the coercive and undemocratic image of the police force as a whole. According to one member of the ethnic squad who had served on the unit for four years: "It's mainly a public relations job."

On the other hand, the Liaison Group on Law Enforcement and Race Relations has been a long-term, financially sound program. Finally, a police commission subcommittee on police-minority relations was established in December 1979 (Bruner, 1981: iii). Unfortunately,

As a result of the impasse reached in the pursuit of community versus police objectives, the committees generally followed a reactive course, examining individual cases of conflict and discussing established police procedures. The uses of the committees as mere forums for the explanation . . . of police practices proved unacceptable to community members and several resigned on the grounds that the committees were "pro-police" and had achieved few practical results. A subsequent restructuring of the project (renamed the "Council on Race Relations and Policing") removed all anarchic tendencies of the local committees by simply abolishing them! (Stasiulis, 1989: 72)

Outcomes

The Evans incident would have been relegated to the dustbin of history had it not been for the police shooting of Albert Johnson, another black man, on August 26, 1979, in his own home. Widespread protest erupted in Toronto's ethnic communities, culminating in September 1979 with the passage by the Toronto City Council of a resolution of nonconfidence in the MTPF. As a result, and perhaps out of fear of a riotous situation similar to the ones witnessed in the United States after police shootings of African Americans, the Police Commission appointed Emmett Cardinal Carter of the Toronto Roman Catholic church as provisional mediator between the police and minorities within Metro.[22] The terms of reference of this appointment were very unclear, and many community leaders in Toronto were highly skeptical. At the end of October 1979, Carter submitted a report (Carter, 1979), well aware that while the board had implemented many of the recommendations of the Morand (Ontario, 1976), Maloney (1975), and Pitman (1977) reports, there was still much to be done. In particular, he wanted the Chief of Police to issue a directive, warning police officers against the use of verbal insults or taunts against citizens; the Commission to establish a committee as a link between them and visible minorities; the reestablishment and development of the use of police foot patrols; the recruitment of more minorities to reflect a broader representation of Toronto's community; the introduction of a point system to aid in the promotion of minorities in the department; a massive education program on racism for officers; and, like those commissioners who had preceded him, an improved procedure for handling complaints against the police, such as a Public Complaints Commissioner (Carter, 1979). It was not until 1981 that the Public Complaints Commissioner's office was finally established. The Progressive Conservative Party could not get the legislation for the creation of the OPCC through the minority government, and they did not want to force it on the police. The legislation, when finally enacted, prompted Lord Scarman of Britain, in his report on the Brixton riots, to suggest that the Ontario legislation was the best in the world. During this time, much was being done to improve community relations between the police and visible minorities, while the board said that money was not available for foot patrols.

At the time of conducting this research, only two of the recommendations were known to be effected. One result was the establishment of a subcommittee of the Police Commission "to meet representatives of various racial and ethnic groups." The group had several meetings a year in the boardroom at Police Headquarters (Bruner, 1981: 82). The board also tried to make the police force reflect the diversity of the community. It began by commissioning John Clement, a Bay Street lawyer, "to examine the recruitment and standards practices" (Clement, 1980). The board followed Clement's recommendations to "advertise for recruits in the ethnic media and to develop a system that removed the former height and weight requirements and substituted a point system to determine the qualification of recruits, which includes height and weight among the factors" (Bruner, 1981: 83).

In sum, the criminal background and intentions of Evans and the "cleanness" of Clark's shooting did not diminish community outcry for change. It would take another shooting of a visible minority (i.e., Albert Johnson), but under more questionable circumstances, for changes in the external control of the police to take place. These controls were finally implemented externally and affected the whole force a decade later, after the passage of the *Police Services Act* (1991).

Torture: Rodney Edward Turner (May 15, 1979)[23]

Rodney Edward Turner, 22, claimed that on May 15, 1979, he was taken to a small room in the 22nd Division Police Station, was ordered to strip, was handcuffed to a chair, was blindfolded, and then had his scrotum ripped open during a police interrogation about an armed robbery that had taken place a couple of days earlier at a Canadian Tire store. Four members of the MTPF police hold-up squad—Sergeants Bert Novis, 49, Patrick Kelly, 47, John Jackson, 45, and Ronald Totty, 24—

were charged by Justice of the Peace Neil Burgess with wounding and assault causing bodily harm to Turner.

Media Initiation

This incident was revealed by a court reporter who covered Turner's initial trial, in two separate stories on subsequent days, approximately 10 days after the alleged incident took place. Almost three months later, when Turner was brought to trial for sentencing, a follow-up story was done, and again nine months later, when the officers went to trial. The majority of articles were written by the *Globe & Mail*'s and *Toronto Star*'s court reporters, Vianney Carriere and Kevin Scanlon, respectively.

Arousal

Beyond the direct participants (the victim and officers accused of the incident, the judge and prosecutor), the incident involved CIRPA. Turner, in a later trial, claimed that he spent eight days in the hospital because of the assault and had to return to the hospital three or four times for follow-up treatment. While Turner's case garnered media attention, it did not provoke much public outcry. Part of the reason might have been that it was overshadowed by the Evans and Johnson inquests, underway at the same time.

Reaction

According to Allan Sparrow, former Alderman and key organizer of the CIRPA, during this period the MTPF stocked the hold-up squad with some of its most hard-bitten cops, whose job was to extract confessions from suspects. They were accused of engaging in Russian roulette, dry-submarining,[24] using false affidavits, and being given carte blanche; all special investigation squads were corrupted in the abuse of power.[25] A change in management sometimes resulted when the police suffered external criticism. The Chief of Police, though, maintained as much distance as he could under the plausible deniability rationale that he did not want to interfere with his investigating officers. The criticisms led the police to gather more objective evidence against suspects for courtroom purposes.[26]

Turner was no saint. He had a history of criminal charges and convictions. He was refused bail, and seven months later he was sentenced to eight years in a penitentiary for armed robbery and assault causing bodily harm. The trial of the officers started in September 1980. In the Supreme Court of Ontario, the officers claimed that Turner was kicked in the groin when he lunged at them during the interrogation. On September 22, 1980, the police were acquitted of the charges. On October 23, Anton Zuraw, a dissatisfied Hamilton Crown attorney who prosecuted the case, said that it was referred to the Ontario Court of Appeal. On October 23, 1981, almost a year later, the acquittal was upheld.[27]

As early as 1981, the CIRPA had recommended that electronic monitoring systems be installed in interrogation rooms.[28] Again, in 1984, long after the fact, Sidney Linden, the first head of the Office of the Public Complaints Commission (OPCC), urged the videotaping of suspects being interviewed to prevent police abuse. Then Deputy Police Chief McCormick said, "The force will join with crown law officers to form a task force on the report, which also urges better supervision of interrogators and record keeping during questioning." This report was mainly in response to continued allegations of abuse by the hold-up squad. The probe by the OPCC was ordered after lawyers complained about abuse to Chief Jack Ackroyd, McMurtry, and Amnesty International. The examination included 23 incidents between May 15, 1979 (the Turner incident), and December 5, 1981. Edward Greenspan, a respected establishment criminal lawyer, was counsel for the hold-up squad during the inquiry.[29] The practice of videotaping suspects, however, was not implemented city wide.

Outcomes

The Turner case on its own did not lead to any discernible change in the types of controls implemented in the police department, yet a subsequent series of similar alleged and actual police-torture incidents forced an external review and the implementation, on a limited basis, of a videotape project.[30]

Police Riot: Morrish Road Incident (May 29, 1982)[31]

On May 29, 1982, 45 people, including 14 policemen, were injured when 53 officers raided a party attended by 300 to 500 young people on Morrish Road in the predominantly WASP Toronto suburb of Scarborough. Party goers were struck with nightsticks, kicked, and then dragged from the front lawn of the house during the confrontation.

Media Initiation

The event was filmed by CITY-TV television cameramen who had been monitoring police scanners at that time, and it was immediately broadcast for the CITY-TV audience. News of the incident then spread to other local media.

Arousal

By the next morning, the mayor, alderpersons, Police Superintendents, and the Chief of Police knew about the incident. Later, the Police Commission, members of the Royal Canadian Mounted Police (RCMP), victims, their friends, families, lawyers, and the CIRPA became involved in the aftermath of the incident.

Reaction

There were both internal and external investigations of this incident. The police subpoenaed the CITY-TV videotape, while Linden headed a public probe into what became labeled as the Morrish Road Incident. According to Jane Pepino, who was on the police commission during this time, "We were all shocked, upset and appalled" with this situation. The commission sent the videotape to the RCMP to be enlarged. However, it was difficult to identify the officers, because the lighting conditions under which the tape was shot were bad, many of the police officers were not wearing their badges, and the officers were lined up in a cordon with their backs to the cameras. According to Pepino,

Jack Ackroyd [then current chief] did not have a good pipeline to the precinct and they did not want to pull in officers. Some people on the commission said the officers were justified. They pulled in the policewoman who was not swinging her baton to see if she would identify the officers who were swinging their batons. It was like asking a female victim of male committed violence to go on the stand. And the view of women in the force at that time was not good.[32]

In an attempt to break up the code of silence, the woman officer was forced to identify the other police involved. By the time the videotapes came back from the RCMP, the commission had transcripts of the radio calls. The commission then called in the superintendents and asked them to account for their actions. Ackroyd tried to lay assault charges but did not have sufficient evidence.[33]

The event took on cult-like proportions, especially when individuals who allegedly were present at the incident, "wore . . . black T-shirts with white letters stating 'I survived the Morrish Road Massacre' " (Ericson, Baranek, and Chan, 1987: 281–282). In April 1983, almost a year after the event, Linden, with three years' experience behind him, recommended that Ackroyd make a general and written apology to victims and individual complainants. He also urged the Chief to offer compensation to citizens claiming property damage. In the meantime, the CIRPA took up the case of five victims who sought compensation for personal injury, time lost from work, and property damage.

Outcomes

On September 3, 1983, Ackroyd publicly admitted that he was "somewhat ashamed and quite appalled" by the conduct of some of his officers. He said that the police who were at the scene that night were retrained in crowd control and proper use of batons.[34] The Chief added that all citizens who complained of mistreatment received written apologies from the force (Harper, 1983). Although some out-of-court settlements amounting to $4,687 were made, no one on the force was disciplined, and no senior officers were held accountable.[35] According to Mark Dailey, the CITY-TV police/crime reporter at the time and current news director, the incident "had a great effect on the police. The force now uses the melee as an example of poor riot control when delivering courses at the police training college."[36] After the event, the police experimented with several community-public relations exercises at an unprecedented rate.

On May 30, 1983, almost a year after the incident, the MTPF, in an effort to allow citizens an opportunity to become involved with the police on an informal basis, opened its first police Mini-Station. According to John Sewell, former mayor and Ward Six Alderman, the location "was not selected because there was any need or any requirement but simply because there was some empty space sitting there."[37] According to Ward Six Alderman Jack Layton, by not having chosen the location based on the criteria that were outlined in a preliminary report, "What they've done is jeopardize the likelihood of the success of this experiment." For Layton and Sewell, Police Mini-Stations would be more effective if they were located in the North Jarvis area. Layton cited this area's unique problem of street prostitution and the hope that "a neighborhood police station would be much less likely to be harassing the Gay community than would the undercover morality squad people."[38]

Joan De Peza, director of the Metro Committee on Race Relations, said that she does not know if Mini-Stations are there to help citizens. "The doors are never open, it is not inviting, and there is some perception that they hassle the local youth." She said the "people are just putting Band-Aids on problems." The Mini-Stations struggled with the perception that if they are like most of the other police-community relations programs instituted by the MTPF, they will either be a form of public relations or fail, due to lack of clear goals and procedures for carrying out tasks.[39]

SUMMARY

Rather than making long-term changes as a result of excessive police violence, the pattern in Toronto follows the British tradition of politicians establishing a flood of commissions and investigative bodies. Genuine policy change was slow and did not come about until a series of incidents of police violence occurred, particularly ones where people were killed by police in a relatively short span of time amid a great deal of rank-and-file resistance to outsider scrutiny.[40] At that, only an external body (i.e., OPCC) was created, which depended on the police for its initial investigation.[41] Changes initiated by the police were usually in the implementation of special community relations units. By the same token, the community voiced negative reactions only after several people of the same race were killed, while criminals were perceived to be getting their just desserts. Only when the public had incontrovertible evidence that police wrongdoing took place were the police motivated to change. These reforms were, however, primarily in the area of internal controls (retraining) or directed at the individual officers who had engaged in the deviant actions (overreacting to a suspect's activities).

The year 1991 was a transitional one because of the election of the Provincial New Democratic Party (NDP) in Ontario (a party that has traditionally been a vocal critic of the police), and the implementation of the *Police Services Act* (Ontario, 1991). Consequently, a new but uncertain era of policing is emerging. Moreover, there is an increasing perception that an inordinate amount of drug-related crime is being committed with weapons, especially by black Jamaicans (posses). This has led to a considerable amount of police lobbying by politically astute senior management to increase their anti-drug efforts. Despite racist labels, McCormick, the Chief chosen in 1989, was called "progressive and proactive" by insiders and outsiders alike.

NOTES

1. Three types of literature have been written on the Metropolitan Toronto Police Force (MTPF): academic, governmental, and journalistic. With respect to academic research, this material can be categorized into studies of reform (McMahon and Ericson, 1984); attitudes of citizens toward the police (Curtis, 1970); public relations efforts (Beare, 1987); police-community service officers (Dunlop and Greenway, 1972); law enforcement-race relations committees (Gandy, 1979); the bathhouse raids (Fleming, 1983); police shootings (Abraham et al., 1981); complaints against police (Henshel, 1983); the self-published autobiography of a retired Chief of Police (Mackey, 1985); the autobiography of a retired Chief of Detectives (Webster, 1991); and history (Rogers, 1984; Boritch, 1985; Boritch and Hagan, 1987; Marquis, 1987).

Alternatively, one can examine a series of Royal Commission reports that were initiated following in the wake of controversial acts of police violence (e.g., Metropolitan Toronto Board of Commissioners, 1970; Ontario, 1972; Ontario, 1976; Pitman, 1977) or private consultant reports (e.g, ARA Consultants, 1985; Hickling-Johnston Ltd., 1982).

Finally, most journalistic writing on the MTPF consists of daily reporting by newspaper journalists and periodic magazine articles appearing in such "lifestyle" magazines as *Toronto Life* or *Saturday Night*. These outlets feature personality pieces on police chiefs, members of the police commission, or successes of the police in foiling particular crimes or crime waves. The majority of this work is primarily descriptive and written for entertainment purposes. Indeed, most of the journalistic research has focused on safe topics. Moreover, this research often depends on the cooperation of the police and the cultivation of special sources in the police department, access which is typically denied to critical outsiders. Although the literature had a respectable beginning, nearly all of it was written during the turbulent 1970s and 1980s, and thus it is time specific. It also did not examine police violence beyond a few case studies.

2. This point is echoed by Betcherman (1982: 17).

3. Based on a personal interview with Allan Sparrow, January 2, 1991.

4. Montréal traditionally and empirically has had the highest number of bank robberies in Canada. Stories, most likely urban legends or myths of ruthless well-armed Québécois bank robbers driving down highway 401 to Toronto to pull off bank jobs, were told to me several times by police personnel.

5. The term *prince of the city* comes from Daley's book (1978) by the same name.

6. The two newspapers, *Globe* and *Mail and Empire*, later amalgamated into the *Globe & Mail*.

7. "Ukrainians to Document Complaints," *The Globe & Mail*, October 28, 1971, p. 5; "City Requests Policy Inquiry," *The Globe & Mail*, October 28, 1971, p. 5.

8. And two days later, on October 27, the Toronto City Council asked the Metro Police Commission for a comprehensive report on the OSC event.

9. Altogether, over 300 people were charged. The raids were viewed by protesters as evidence of ongoing systematic police harassment of the gay community. Critics of the raids made reference to previous incidents which included, between 1977 and 1979, the laying of charges of publishing "immoral, indecent or scurrilous material" against *The Body Politic*, a newspaper for the gay community, the Barracks bathhouse raids, informing school boards that their employees were gay, and the use of entrapment techniques in public washrooms. Critics of the raid called for a public inquiry and also drew attention once more to previous calls for reform of various aspects of policing. See Fleming (1983) for a review of the bathhouse raids. See White and Sheppard (1981) for a quasipolitical interpretation. See Harry Sutherland's documentary "Track Two" by KLS Communications (1982) for another interpretation of the situation.

10. Based on a review of government documents and a series of interviews with Harold Adamson, Howard Moscoe, Philip Givens, Jack Layton, Clare Lewis, Roy McMurtry, Jane Pepino, Allan Sparrow, and Paul Walter.

11. Information concerning these controls was garnered through a series of interviews with sources.

12. Two commissions have been ordered to inquire into the MTPF. The first was the "Royal Commission of Inquiry in Relation to the Conduct of the Public and The Metropolitan Toronto Police," supervised by Judge Ilvio Anthony Vannini (Ontario, 1972). The second was the "Royal Commission of Inquiry into Metropolitan Toronto Police Practices," conducted by Justice Donald Morand (Ontario, 1976). Two reports have been conducted on behalf of City Hall. The first was the 1970 inquiry conducted by Judge C. O. Bick. The second was the 1971 review of citizen complaint procedures headed by criminal lawyer Arthur Maloney.

13. "Weight of police officer," and "Weight of victim," were not included, because all values are missing. "Morality of the setting" was not included, as most incidents lacked this component.

14. "National police organizations," "businesses and their associations," and "police union/association," were dropped because all of the information was missing.

15. Although the Albert Johnson shooting (August 26, 1979) received a considerable number of newspaper citations (27), a similar New York City case garnering a sufficient number of stories could not be found, hence this incident was not omitted from intensive analysis.

16. This event shares a number of similarities with the NYC Perry shooting: both victims were young and black, it involved two brothers, one of whom was shot by a white policeman, and it occurred in a public place.

17. Based on personal interviews with friends of Evans, who wished to remain anonymous, on June 29, 1990.

18. Based on a personal interview with Mal Conolly on March 14, 1991.

19. Michael Keating, "Bail Is Granted to Allow Evans to Attend Slain Brother's Funeral," *Globe & Mail*, August 12, 1978, p. 14; "40 Protest Against Killing of Black Man by Constable," *Globe & Mail*, August 10, 1978.

20. Based on a personal interview with Charles Roach on July 30, 1990.

21. Arthur Johnson, "Lawyers Trade Shouts, Evans Inquest Interrupted," *Globe & Mail*, May 15, 1979, p. 5; Arthur Johnson, "Evans Made Death Threat Previous Day, Inquest Told," *Globe & Mail*, May 16, 1979, p. 2; Arthur Johnson, "Evans Had Hands Up Before Slaying, Jury Told," *Globe & Mail*, May 17, 1979, p. 5; Arthur Johnson, "Tavern Bouncer's Statement Altered by Police Officer, Evans Inquest Told," *Globe & Mail*, May 23, 1979, p. 1; Arthur Johnson, "Kicked by Police, Evans Brother Says," *Globe & Mail*, May 26, 1979, p. 4; Arthur Johnson. "Shouting of Lawyers Overshadows Inquiry into Evans Shooting," *Globe & Mail*, May 28, 1979, p. 5; Arthur Johnson, "Report Differs on Weapon Used by Buddy Evans," *Globe & Mail*, May 30, 1979, p. 4; "Brutality Probe Would Hamper Inquest: Crown," *Globe & Mail*, May 30, 1979, p. 4; Arthur Johnson, "Inquest Lawyers Disbelieve Story of Police Beating," *Globe & Mail*, May 31, 1979, p. 5; Arthur Johnson, "Policeman Said Obscenity to Woman, Evans Trial Is Told," *Globe & Mail*, June 2, 1979, p. 5; Arthur Johnson, "Police Brutality Not Your Issue Evans Jury Told," *Globe & Mail*, June 5, 1977, p. 5; Arthur Johnson, "Evans Inquest Hearing Closed, Ministry Wants to Know Why," *Globe & Mail*, June 7, 1979, p. 1; Yves Lavigne, "Realized Only in Hospital Evans Dead, Officer Says," *Globe & Mail*, June 7, 1979, p. 13; Arthur Johnson, "Had Headaches Weeks after Being Clubbed by Buddy Evans, Constable Tells Inquest," *Globe & Mail*, June 8, 1979, p. 5; Arthur Johnson, "Lawyer Escapes Charge in Dispute on Testimony," *Globe & Mail*, June 9, 1979, p. 5; Ross Laver, "Evans Punched, Kicked Officer in Nova Scotia, Inquest Is Told," *Globe & Mail*, August 30, 1979, p. 5; Ross Laver, "Knew Constable Would Kill One Day, Man Tells Inquest," *Globe & Mail*, August 31, 1979; Ross Laver, "Dispatcher Was Demoted for Racism, Inquest Told," *Globe & Mail*, September 5, 1979, p. 5; Ross Laver, "Evans Inquest Halted after Lawyer Walks Out," *Globe & Mail*, September 14, 1979, p. 44; Ross Laver, "Evans Had Criminal Record from Age of 16, Jury Told," *Globe & Mail*, September 15, 1979, p. 5; James Jefferson, "The Lawyer at the Centre of the Evans Inquest Controversy," *Globe & Mail*, October 3, 1979, p. 3; "Evans Jury Urges Changes in Police Practices," *Globe & Mail*, October 4, 1979, p. 5; Ross Laver and Julia Turner, "Officer Cleared in Evans Death," *Globe & Mail*, October 4, 1979, pp. 1–2; Julia

Turner, "Coroner Accused of Denying Basic Rights after Evans Lawyer Refused Adjournment," *Globe & Mail*, October 5, 1979; "Advice from the Jury in Evans Case," *Globe & Mail*, October 5, 1979, p. 6; and "No Probes by Outsiders—Police Chief Adamson to Evans Jury Recommendation," *Globe & Mail* November 30, 1979, p. 1.

22. Christie Blatchford, "Metro Police Chief Denies Racist Charges," *Toronto Star*, September 1, 1979, pp. A1–A2; Alden Baker, "Cardinal to Mediate Racial Tension Caused by Metro Police," *Globe & Mail*, September 7, 1979, pp. 1–2; "Jewish Leaders Want Probe of Police Violence," *Toronto Star*, October 3, 1979, p. A-3; Janice Dineen, "Reform the Police Alderman Demand," *Toronto Star*, October 5, 1979, pp. A1, A2; Michael McAteer, "Eight Arrested as 1,200 Hold Rally Against Racism and Police Violence," *Toronto Star*, October 15, 1979, p. A-3.

23. This incident is similar to the Davidson event, because both of the "victims" were white, both had a criminal record or were charged with a criminal offense, and the torture was applied to the subjects' testicles. The Turner incident must be taken in the context of a series of torture incidents that the hold-up squad was accused of. In one noteworthy event, the hold-up squad was defended by Edward Greenspan, a well-known, respected Toronto criminal lawyer.

24. The practice of placing an individual's head underwater (e.g., in a tank or a toilet), which makes it difficult to breath and simulates the sensation of drowning.

25. Based on a personal interview with Allan Sparrow on January 2, 1990.

26. Ibid.

27. Kevin Scanlon, "4 Metro Officers Accused of Police Station Assault," *Toronto Star*, May 25, 1979, p. A-3; "4 Metro Policemen Charged with Assault," *Globe & Mail*, May 26, 1979, p. 9; "Man Who Accused Police of Brutality Gets 8 Years," *Toronto Star*, December 4, 1979, p. A-23; "8 Years for Robbery, Assault," *Globe & Mail*, December 4, 1979, p. 5; "Assault Alleged Four Policemen Will Stand Trial," *Globe & Mail*, December 13, 1979, p. 11; "4 Policemen on Trial in Wounding," *Toronto Star*, September 9, 1980, p. A-3; "Officers Plead Not Guilty," *Globe & Mail*, September 9, 1980, p. xx; Vianney Carriere, "Tortured by Police, Man 24, Testifies," *Globe & Mail*, September 10, 1980, p. 5; Vianney Carriere, "Brutality Charge Not Play, Robber Says," *Globe & Mail*, September 11, 1980, p. 4; Vianney Carriere, "2 Officers Threatened Charges over Allegation, Lawyer Says," *Globe & Mail*, September 16, 1980, p. 3; Vianney Carriere, "Prisoner Kicked in Groin after Attacking Officer, Two Policemen Testify," *Globe & Mail*, September 17, 1980, p. 4; Vianney Carriere, "4 Metro Police Officers Acquitted on Charges of Assaulting Suspect," *Globe & Mail*, September 23, 1980, p. 5; "Torture Acquittals Questioned," *Toronto Star*, October 24, 1980, p. A3; "Officers' Assault Acquittal Upheld by Court of Appeal," *Toronto Star*, October 24, 1980, p. A-3.

28. Sally McBeth, "CIRPA Alleges Police Torture," *Toronto Clarion*, November 6, 1981, p. 7.

29. Cal Miller, "Tape Suspects to Curb Abuse, Police Urged," *Toronto Star*, April 7, 1984, pp. A1–A4.

30. According to Jack Gemmell, "The video projects are show trials. Homicide has gotten into it. They bring someone in and he fesses up. They then get a statement from them. Then they ask the guy if he wants to repeat it in front of a video. Taking statements from complainants (particularly sexual assault) pre-

vents them from withdrawing it." Based on a personal interview on April 7, 1991.

31. This incident is similar to the Tompkins Square event because both were videotaped, it was eventually subpoenaed, and it involved primarily white victims who launched complaints with the official and unofficial complaint organizations.

32. Based on a personal interview with Jane Pepino on April 5, 1991.

33. Ibid.

34. Ackroyd was perceived by some in his department as a "bleeding heart," and this may have been one of the reasons he took an early retirement. Others have said that he liked a high lifestyle, and that, at the time the study was conducted, is one of the reasons he was suffering medical problems. Ackroyd has passed away since research was conducted for this study.

35. Based on a personal interview with Harold Levy on March 14, 1991.

36. Based on a personal interview with the author on June 10, 1983.

37. Ibid.

38. Ibid.

39. ARA Consultants (1985).

40. In other words, the only change was the implementation of the office of the public complaints commissioner, an external control.

41. According to Sparrow, the fastest change was the physical identification of police in the force (i.e., badge numbers on their hats). Sparrow outlines how he, in his capacity as a city alderman, wrote to all of the major police forces in the world to determine their regulations in this policy area. He presented his findings to the police. "It took a year and the force came back with a report. There is a provincial insecurity and anything that is comparative is helpful. Taking Toronto cops to Detroit or Los Angeles is instructive."

Chapter 4

The Politics and Control of
Police Violence in New York City

It is a short bus ride from Newark International Airport to New York City's Port Authority terminal. The bus winds its way around the airport terminal, exits onto the New Jersey Turnpike and goes through the airport strip district, which is replete with well-known hotel chains, warehouses, and light industry that spring up in these areas throughout North America. The bus stops at a toll booth, then brushes by downtown Newark across the elevated highway, goes through the Lincoln Tunnel, and winds itself across a short stretch of blocks to the terminal. Once off the bus and in the Port Authority terminal, visitors are psychologically overwhelmed by a barrage of street people offering to carry their bags or looking for a handout, scenes almost reminiscent of a third-world country.

The tension is both palpable and unmistakable. New York City police routinely patrol the terminal, ensuring that everything stays under control. "Keeping a lid on things" has several unwritten rules, including issuing a warning to transients to smacking their heads as long as no one powerful enough to protest witnesses it. This form of persuasion is by no means exceptional; it is part of the repertoire that New York City Police Department (NYPD) officers and other law enforcement personnel employ to deal with one of the most stressful jobs ever created. Despite this reality, police violence in New York City must be placed in the wider context of the history of policing in the Big Apple.

HISTORY OF REACTIONS TO POLICE VIOLENCE IN NEW YORK CITY[1]

There is perhaps no better place in America to study policing than New York City. It has the largest police department, the highest police-to-citizen ratio, and one of the oldest police forces in the United States. Indeed, the NYPD is a microcosm of big-city police throughout America. Like other departments, the NYPD has responded in a variety of ways to an increasingly diverse population, to changing crime, to financial constraints, and to reforms, including controls instituted in response to corruption and police violence. Even though the NYPD is probably the most researched police force in the world, there are several obstacles to conducting objective research on the force.[2]

Police violence has historically been a significant problem in New York City. Violence has been directed toward indigents, minorities, strikers, and demonstrators, among others. In fact, violence toward New York's indigents and African-American populations predates the organization of the force; it was committed by the military, which originally assumed policing functions. Although these acts have been documented elsewhere, information on how the community of concern has responded is unconsolidated.

The NYPD was created in 1844, when the New York State Legislature passed a law abolishing the watch in New York City and created a single, unified day and night police. Under the new plan, the Chief of Police was appointed by the mayor, and the captains and patrolmen were chosen for one-year terms by city ward leaders.[3] Since the very first police took to the streets of New York City, the community of concern has generally reacted in six principal ways.

1. During the nineteenth century, *sections of the public* (i.e., the middle class) *approved of police brutality*, particularly in connection with labor disputes and parades (Miller, 1977: 51–52, 195). The Draft or "great" riots of 1863, for example, involved four days of anti-black riots initiated by Irish New Yorkers. The police, using clubs and guns, "contained the rioting and became heroes to New Yorkers, who believed they had saved the city from an Irish lumpen proletariat émeute" (Miller, 1977: 22). This only increased the "hostility between the police and many of the slum dwellers." During this time, "Policemen developed an almost pathological insistence on respect, considering violence as [a] legitimate and even morally necessary way of dealing with those who did not exhibit the proper deference to them" (p. 158).[4] "Middle-class commentators praised the police for their discipline and their courage and noted the way 'locusts' [i.e., police clubs] fell on rioters' heads . . . they did not speculate on whether there was any other way to deal with riots and rioters" (p. 143).

2. *Newspapers reported and voiced opinions about police violence*. For instance, in July 1871, "during a Orangeist parade, a riot took place and someone fired a shot, prompting the militia to fire into the crowd, killing and wounding more than one hundred people. . . . [One newspaper] criticized the police for their indiscriminate cracking of heads" (Miller, 1977:

166–167). In the twentieth century, the "tough cops" of the 1930s, such as John James Broderick, attracted headlines for their bravery and unorthodox (violent) methods. Gerald Astor says, "the tough cop had been one answer for an openly lawless period. But the tough cop had no influence upon hidden corruption. At best the Brodericks forced gangsters to be more discreet." In 1930, an unlawful assembly of 35,000 to 50,000 communists at Union Square ended up with police "flailing nightsticks." Newspaper reports of the event suggested that the police acted as agent provocateurs and prevented newsreel footage of the violence (Astor, 1971: 169–170).

3. *Officers were charged with, and in some cases convicted of, criminal offenses* in connection with police violence. For example, in 1858, "Sailor Jack," an Irish longshoreman who was considered dangerous and disorderly, was shot by Patrolman Cairnes. Consequently, this led to the "arrest, imprisonment, and dismissal of charges against him" (Astor, 1971: 146–147).

After the turn of the century, a constant stream of incidents of police violence (including blackjack beatings and shootings by officers) occurred, resulting in assault or murder charges against the police. Around 1910, several of these incidents were reported in the papers. In particular, in 1912, Lieutenant Charles Becker, of the "Strong Arms Squad," murdered Herman Rosenthal, a gambling house owner who had implicated him in corruption charges. "Becker and four of his colleagues were found guilty and sentenced to the electric chair" (Astor, 1971: 115).

4. *Police shootings of citizens under questionable circumstances led to rioting.* Ghetto violence in New York City in 1964, 1967, and 1968 resulted from several incidents of police violence. For instance, in July 1964, the police shooting of James Powell, an African-American youth, and the subsequent police reaction, led to riots in the ghettos of Harlem in Manhattan and Bedford Stuyvesant in Brooklyn.[5] In the summer of 1967, the Puerto Rican community rose in anger, after a police officer shot a knife-wielding youth. Subsequent rioting was accompanied by looting in East Harlem. In the end, "when quiet was restored, two Puerto Ricans had died of bullets fired by police" (Astor, 1971: 177). Moreover, at the trial of three Black Panthers, in 1968, a melee broke out between supporters of the Panthers and off-duty police who were in attendance.

5. *Commissions of inquiry examined, in whole or in part, police use of excessive force.* For example, the 1884 Lexow Committee investigations into corruption and vice in New York City also focused on police brutality. The Committee uncovered a number of police officers who meted out violence so frequently that they were collectively called "the clubbers." Part of the findings revealed that, "even when policemen were convicted of brutality by the commissioners . . . they received lesser punishments than they would have for violations of the rules" (Miller, 1977: 193).

Later on, between 1910 and the early 1930s, "several local and national commissions were created that dealt either wholly or partly with police problems" (Center for the Research of Criminal Justice, 1977: 32).

According to the Center for the Research of Criminal Justice (CRCJ),

[t]he progressives aimed to replace the traditional police reliance on fear and brute force with an increased use of technology. During the 19th century, . . . the police had become identified in the public mind as a club-swinging, brutal organization at the service of special interests. But the use of force, except as a last resort, was counterproductive. . . . Progressive police writings were filled with case histories showing how the unwise use of force in strikes and riots has unwittingly aided the cause of radical "elements." (pp. 36–37)

For example, on March 19, 1935, Lino Rivera, a young African-American man, was accused of stealing a knife from a store in Harlem. A policeman was summoned. Unfounded rumors that the boy had died at the officer's hands provoked a public disorder situation later known as the Harlem riots. During the incident, "Patrolman John McInery shot and fatally wounded Lloyd Hobbs," Patrolman Zabutinski was accused of killing Edward Laurie, and "Thomas Aiken lost an eye during a police scuffle" (Astor, 1971: 171–172).

Following the Harlem riots, a commission appointed by the mayor reported widespread police brutality, including mutilation and murder, against African Americans.[6] Later, in 1947, the President's Commission on Civil Rights condemned widespread police brutality.[7] In 1967, the National Crime Commission reported that excessive brutality was still a "significant problem."[8] And in 1968, the Kerner Commission devoted considerable effort to a series of proposals curtailing police brutality (United States, 1968b).

6. Finally, and most frequently, *complaints were voiced by victims to the police department, elected representatives, and the mass media.* During the 1840s and 1850s, "[T]here were relatively few complaints about the abuse of police authority." Although there was little press coverage of police violence at that time, this can be interpreted in a variety of different ways. One observer of this period commented that "any victim may not have had access to the press or important political figures, but most likely, there was not much brutality" (Miller, 1977, p. 157). Between 1857 and 1870, street fights among police and citizens were common (Richardson, 1970: 110), and "charges of police brutality were made almost daily" (Miller, 1977: 158). "One of the earliest occasions of police use of firearms [was] the seventeenth ward German riot of July 1857," sparked when the police tried to enforce Sunday closing laws "in which an innocent bystander was fatally shot" (p. 195). "[T]he Germans who lived in this area accused the police of being unduly harsh, of using their clubs

indiscriminately and of shooting to death an innocent man" (p. 110). According to Miller (1977),

in the late 1860s policemen used their clubs too freely and occasionally shot unarmed men. By 1868 complaints of brutality had mounted to new heights as had charges that the commissioners had become excessively lax in dealing with such cases. Citizens were often deterred from accusing a policeman because of the indignities they were likely to suffer at the hands of the commissioners. (p. 158)

One century later, in 1953, the FBI publicly announced that its New York office had difficulty investigating the NYPD. "Hoping to capitalize on the poor publicity attendant upon the case, the NYCLU [New York Civil Liberties Union] suggested that the police set up a Civilian Police Review Board." The department readily accepted the proposal but modified it enough to eliminate features deemed necessary by the [NYCLU]" (Astor, 1971: 228). Complaints concerning police violence climbed during the 1950s and early 1960s and "ranged from simple absence of respect toward minority group members to out-and-out physical beatings, including several incidents that ended with the deaths of civilians" (Astor, 1971: 228). In many incidents, victims or their families filed charges against the police department. For example, "In the early 1960s two thugs mortally wounded a pair of policemen. . . . Detectives seeking information learned of a small-time Brooklyn hood who might have some knowledge about the killings. . . . Later, the defendant's lawyer filed an appeal claiming that the witness had been coerced into revealing vital information. As part of the appeal court records the defense lawyer showed that the police had stubbed out cigarettes on their informant's testicles" (Astor, 1971).

During the 1960s, the Tactical Police Force (TPF), created in 1959 and comprising "a unit of men specially selected for brains, brawn, and willingness to work difficult situations," was accused of police violence. "Not all of the public saw in the TPF unmixed virtue. Several times ghetto people accused them of swinging too free and eager a club, precipitating wider violence than might have normally occurred" (Astor, 1971: 204). The TPF was the source of numerous complaints, because "whenever street demonstrations, picketing, or civil disturbances occur, . . . its members serve[d] as shock troops and as the first barrier of containment. Some observers believe[d] that the emphasis upon 'enforcement' for the men of the TPF promotes a tendency for them to swing their nightsticks too soon. These critics feel that TPF behavior turns tension into street battles" (Astor, 1971: 205). In the spring of 1968, "after several weeks of protesting over the erection of a new University gymnasium that would use a piece of city park land on the edge of the

Harlem ghetto, some three-hundred Columbia students seized Hamilton Hall, . . . [and] more than twenty plainclothesmen, armed with night sticks, attempted to liberate the president's office." On the eighth day, some of the demonstrators who were departing from an occupied building were injured. "The night ended with 720 people arrested . . . and 149 injured. . . . Many complaints were filed on police brutality" (pp. 193–194). One month later, Hamilton Hall was seized again by students, and the police were called in. This led to a near-riot situation; many students were injured in the ensuing melee. In the end, there were "135 arrests, 51 student injuries, and 17 police injuries" (p. 196).

CONTROLLING THE NYPD

In response to the public disclosure of celebrated acts of corruption, police violence, and abuses of authority, controls on the NYPD emerged and evolved. Currently, the NYPD is controlled both internally and externally through a variety of mechanisms found in most other major police departments, however, a number of features are unique to the NYPD in this regard.

Internal Mechanisms

Currently, the police department has three tiers: personnel, management, and operational support, which are coordinated at headquarters, located at 1 Police Plaza, close to City Hall. Conterminously, there are five major bureaus of the NYPD: field services, detectives, organized crime control, personnel, and inspectorial. Within field services, there are seven patrol boroughs. Furthermore, Manhattan and Brooklyn are each subdivided, thereby creating a total of 75 precincts that are "responsible for police services and protection of approximately 319.8 square miles and approximately eight million people" (Reuss-Ianni, 1984: 23).[9] The population in each precinct ranges between 100,000 and 125,000 citizens. In general, there are six major internal controls. They are (in increasing order of importance): the alcoholism and counseling section, standing orders, policies, Trials Department, Internal Affairs Bureau (IAB), and Police Commissioner.[10]

External Mechanisms

External mechanisms can be divided between governmental and public mechanisms. The following three major governmental external controls on the NYPD exist: the Citizen's/Civilian Review Board (CCRB), the Chief Medical examiner, and the grand juries and the District Attor-

Table 4.1
**Comparison of Allegations of Police Violence Based on Different
Organizations and Classification**

Year	CCRB[a]	Public Police Violence[b]
1977	2,295	2
1978	2,528	0
1979	2,030	3
1980	1,929	5
1981	unknown	1
1982	2,761	0
1983	3,024	7
1984	3,525	7
1985	3,538	7
1986	3,303	4
1987	3,106	7
1988	4,178	9
1989	3,515	3
1990		9
Missing		1
	-----	-----
TOTAL		65

a. Complaints of police excessive force. Despite personal visits and a year's worth of correspondence, the CCRB only sent me two annual reports from which I was able to determine four years' worth of statistics. The statistics between 1977 and 1985 were made available by William Wilkins, Associate Staff Analyst, July 1991, personal correspondence.
b. Based on *New York Times* coverage only.

ney.[11] On the other hand, there are two principal types of public external controls on the NYPD: various police unions and the mass media.[12]

RESULTS FROM EPISODE CHARACTERISTICS, REACTION, AND OUTCOME VARIABLES

History, controls, and perceptions of police violence aside, empirical evidence of police violence during the 14-year period was examined. As with the Toronto case, 23 attributes, including single and/or combinations of variables from the public police violence (PPV) data set, are explored in this section.

Episode Characteristics

If relying on the CCRB or PPV statistics, New York City has consistently experienced an increase in the annual level of police violence (see Table 4.1). According to the PPV data, the rise had been somewhat moderate from 1977 until the beginning of the 1980s; from about 1982 onward, the increase was somewhat sharper, accounting for most (83%) of

Table 4.2
Severity (degree of harm to victim)

	Frequency	Percent
Torture	3	4.6
Deadly Force (may or may not result in death)	5	7.7
Brutality (unspecified/misc.)	13	20.0
Beating (includes assault)	18	27.7
Killing (unspecified)	25	38.5
Missing	1	1.5
	-----	-----
TOTAL	65	100.0

the cases. Although the increase has not been steady, the trend was definitely upward, peaking in 1980, 1983 to 1985, and 1987 to 1989. It is interesting to note that in the wake of these peaks, a sharp drop in the number of police violence acts was recorded. This decline suggests (among other things) that, following incidents of well-publicized police violence, either police officers' use of violence in citizen encounters is reduced and more "controlled," or media attention and public outcry has waned (e.g., this could be part of an issue attention cycle effect).[13] Even when the force is under new mayoral (e.g., Edward Koch) or Police Chief (e.g., Patrick Murphy and Benjamin Ward) administrations,[14] differences are minimal. It is important to remember, though, that annual trends are only rough consolidations of more intricate patterns.

The bulk of the 65 episodes of public police violence consisted of unspecified killings of citizens by police officers (38%); the second-place positions go to brutality and beatings (20% and 28%, respectively). The number of cases involving some type of torture was minimal (5%) (see Table 4.2).

Since the age differences between the police officers and the victims and the weight of the victims and police officers were missing from most cases, they were excluded from this analysis. On the other hand, it should be noted that the majority (86%) of people affected by police violence were ordinary citizens; only a few (12%) were public figures (see Table 4.3).

Of the cases that could be identified, the bulk of victims were male (74%), interacting with male police officers (59%) (see Table 4.4). Of those incidents coded, 29 percent of the victims were visible minorities, compared to only 5 percent of police officers who were classified in this category. Meanwhile, Caucasian victims compromised 9 percent of the total (see Table 4.5). Moreover, roughly 75 percent of the cases led to a criminal charge being laid against the police officers (see Table 4.6), an action believed to play a large role in convincing the public and govern-

Table 4.3
Status of Victim[a]

	Frequency	Percent
Yes	8	12.3
No	56	86.2
Missing	1	1.5
	-----	-----
TOTAL	65	100.0

a. Whether or not victim was a public figure.

Table 4.4
Gender of Participants

	Victims		Police Officers	
	Frequency	Percent	Frequency	Percent
Female	5	7.7	2	3.1
Male	48	73.8	38	58.5
Mixed	1	1.5		
Missing	11	16.9	25	38.5
	-----	-----	-----	-----
TOTAL	65	100.0	65	100.0

Percentages do not equal 100 due to rounding.

Table 4.5
Race of Participants

	Victims		Police Officers	
	Frequency	Percent	Frequency	Percent
White	6	9.2	8	12.3
Visible minority	19	29.2	3	4.6
Missing	40	61.5	54	83.1
	-----	-----	-----	-----
TOTAL	65	100.0	65	100.0

Percentages do not equal 100 due to rounding.

Table 4.6
Perception of Illegality of Case

	Frequency	Percent
Criminal charge was not discussed	4	6.2
Undetermined	5	7.7
Criminal charge against officer/s was discussed[a]	49	75.4
Missing	7	10.8
	-----	-----
TOTAL	65	100.0

Percentages do not equal 100 due to rounding.

Table 4.7
Number of Participants

No.	Victims Frequency	Percent	Police Officers Frequency	Percent
1	50	76.9	32	49.2
2	8	12.3	8	12.3
3	1	1.5	1	1.5
4	0	0.0	0	0.0
5	0	0.0	3	4.6
6	2	3.1	1	1.5
7	0	0.0	0	0.0
8	0	0.0	1	1.5
Missing	4	6.2	19	29.2
TOTAL	65	100.0	65	100.0

Percentages do not equal 100 due to rounding.

Table 4.8
Demeanor of Subject

	Frequency	Percent
Intoxicated	2	3.1
Mentally ill	5	7.7
Missing	58	89.2
TOTAL	65	100.0

ment officials of the illegality of a particular officer's action, which motivates officials to respond.

Turning to the number of victims, of those cases recorded, the majority (77%) had only one victim, 12 percent had two, and only 3 percent had six (see Table 4.7). The relatively small number of victims involved in each incident may contribute to the public's perception that the event was not as serious as it could have been, thus dulling their reaction. Likewise, almost half of the cases had only one officer involved; only two incidents involved six or more officers.

Although it might seem futile to comment on the demeanor of the victim, since most information regarding their physical or mental status was missing (see Table 4.8), this in itself may be interesting. For example, either the victims were sober and only a small percentage of the victims (2% to 5%) were intoxicated or mentally ill, or this was an item journalists do not think of inquiring about, or editorial decisions have excluded them from the final edition. Furthermore, of those cases coded for victim's type of behavior, 34 percent were passive, offering no resistance to arrest (see Table 4.9). The fact that the majority of victims were sober and passive should increase the public perception of wrongdoing by the officer in question, deeming his or her actions as unnecessary and brutal

Table 4.9
Activity Level of Victim

	Frequency	Percent
Victim was active[b]	8	12.3
Victim carried weapon[c]	9	13.8
Victim was passive[a]	22	33.8
Missing	26	40.0
	-----	-----
TOTAL	65	100.0

a. Includes handcuffed and fleeing.
b. Put up resistance.
c. Includes fake.
Percentages do not equal 100 due to rounding.

Table 4.10
Number of Articles that the Incident Generated

No. of Articles	Frequency	Percent
8	1	1.5
10	1	1.5
11	1	1.5
17	1	1.5
53	1	1.5
55	1	1.5
4	2	3.1
5	2	3.1
6	2	3.1
3	6	9.2
2	8	12.3
1	39	60.0
	-----	-----
TOTAL	65	100.0

Percentages do not equal 100 due to rounding.

and thereby casting a shadow of helplessness around the victims, re-gardless of his or her criminal culpability.

Reaction Variables[15]

With the exception of two celebrated incidents that generated an average of 54 stories, the majority of incidents (60%) garnered only one article printed in the *New York Times*. This implies that most of the cases involving police abuse go unnoticed by the public (see Table 4.10) due to the lack of coverage of these events. In terms of the number of citations, the incidents of police violence that received the most mention were the events discussed by the Conyers Commission (54) (May 5, 1983, to May 21, 1987); the South Ozone Stun Gun incidents (51) (April 19,

Table 4.11
Days Elapsed between First and Last Article on Incident

Days	Frequency	Percent
0	42	64.6
1	1	1.5
3	1	1.5
7	1	1.5
10	1	1.5
14	1	1.5
20	1	1.5
34	1	1.5
43	2	3.1
48	1	1.5
92	1	1.5
100	1	1.5
120	1	1.5
168	1	1.5
181	1	1.5
225	1	1.5
587	1	1.5
740	1	1.5
759	1	1.5
1,262	1	1.5
1,431	1	1.5
1,458	1	1.5
1,971	1	1.5
TOTAL	65	100.0

Percentages do not equal 100 due to rounding.

1985); and the shooting of Edmund Perry (17) (June 13, 1985). The Tompkins Square incident (10) (August 7, 1988) and the Wilson event (11) (November 1, 1988) hold the fourth and fifth positions, respectively. Although the incidents investigated by the Conyers Commission are interesting, they are not easily disaggregated and comparable to any case in Toronto, and they were therefore dropped from the in-depth case study analysis. A number of other controversial events also occurred during this time, including the deaths at the hands of the police, or while in police custody, of Ralph Tarantino (August 24, 1980), Michael Stewart (September 15, 1983), Eleanor Bumpers (October 29, 1984), and Jose Llopes (December 17, 1984).[16] These cases, however, never garnered the same amount of media attention as the ones mentioned above, and hence, they were also excluded.[17]

Not surprisingly, most of the incidents of police violence (65%) received no follow-up articles, as inferred from the days lapsed between the first and last article written about them (see Table 4.11). In terms of scope, while almost half of the cases had missing information, the largest number of outside actors who were involved was 13 (see Table 4.12), but this occurred for only 1.5 percent of the cases recorded; the majority (53%) had only one to 10 such actors involved.

Table 4.12
Scope[a]

No. of People	Frequency	Percent
1	18	27.7
2	4	6.2
3	8	12.3
4	2	3.1
10	1	1.5
13	1	1.5
Missing	31	47.7
	-----	-----
TOTAL	65	100.0

a. Refers to the number of actors who got involved in the incident after it took place.

Table 4.13
Police Union/Association Reaction

	Frequency	Percent
Threatens injunction to block measure	3	4.6
Demonstration in support of officer on trial	1	1.5
Missing	61	93.8
	-----	-----
TOTAL	65	100.0

Percentages do not equal 100 due to rounding.

Although a lot of information was missing from the Police Union/Association variable, 5 percent of the cases coded involved threats of injunction from this type of organization (see Table 4.13). The lack of information (thus coded missing) may suggest either an absence of resistance by the Police Union/Association or a subtle admission of compliance on their part.

Elected officials were relatively passive in their response to incidents of public police violence: in only 22 percent of the incidents cited did they express some type of response to these actions (see Table 4.14).

With respect to citizen reactions, the number of public demonstrations was generally low; only 6 percent of the cases generated some kind of public assembly, while 5 percent had interest groups involved (see Table 4.15). Again, this must be interpreted with caution, because most information was missing.

The media reaction to these types of events overall was weak. Indeed, in only 2 percent of cases did journalists support the police action (see Table 4.16). Moreover, this same pattern of results applies to the victims, governmental agencies, and accused officers' reactions (see Tables 4.17, 4.18, 4.19, respectively). The most common behavior taken by the vic-

Table 4.14
Elected Officials' Reactions

	Frequency	Percent
Incident probed by D.A.	1	1.5
Mayor comments/complains against police	1	1.5
Mayor/state official requests investigation	1	1.5
D.A. accuses police of wrongdoing	1	1.5
Assemblyperson questions police discipline	1	1.5
City council urges hiring new recruits	2	3.1
Representative criticizes police work	2	3.1
Investigation by D.A.	5	7.7
Missing	51	78.5
TOTAL	65	100.0

Percentages do not equal 100 due to rounding.

Table 4.15
Citizens Group/Organization Reactions

	Frequency	Percent
Interest groups call for public inquiry	1	1.5
Residents demand reinstatement of officer(s)	1	1.5
Interest group(s) complains	3	4.6
Public demonstration	4	6.2
Citizens (non-victims) complain	4	6.2
Missing	52	80.0
TOTAL	65	100.0

Table 4.16
Media Reaction

	Frequency	Percent
Journalist supports police action	1	1.5
Proposing citizens on police board	1	1.5
Criticizes unwillingness of police	1	1.5
Neutrally describes event	1	1.5
Says citizen interest group must be heard	1	1.5
Missing	60	92.3
TOTAL	65	100.0

Percentages do not equal 100 due to rounding.

Table 4.17
Victims' and Victims' Relatives' Reaction

	Frequency	Percent
Tells story to the newspaper	1	1.5
Hires lawyer	1	1.5
Launches complaint (misc.)	1	1.5
Lays charge against police officer	3	4.6
Sues police/launches civil action	4	6.2
Missing	55	84.6
	-----	-----
TOTAL	65	100.0

Percentages do not equal 100 due to rounding.

Table 4.18
Government Agencies' Reaction

	Frequency	Percent
CCJJ[a] awards victim financial compensation	1	1.5
Charges are dropped	1	1.5
Grand Jury acquits officer	1	1.5
Sentences officer and awards victim financial compensation	1	1.5
CCJJ lays charge and Grand Jury investigates	1	1.5
CCJJ sentences officer	1	1.5
U.S. Attorney office probes allegation	2	3.1
CCJJ convicts officer of some charges	2	3.1
CCJJ lays charge	6	9.2
CCJJ acquits officer of all charges	12	18.5
Missing	37	56.9
	-----	-----
TOTAL	65	100.0

a. CCJJ means crown, courts, judge, or jury.
Percentages do not equal 100 due to rounding.

tim(s) was to launch a legal action against the police (6%). On the other hand, the most common reaction by government agencies (i.e., crown, courts, judge, or jury) was to acquit the officer in question; only 9 percent of the events resulted in a charge against the officer. And, not surprisingly, the police officer's most common response (5%) was to hire a lawyer to defend himself which, coupled with the CCJJ (crown, courts, judge or jury) action to acquit officers, makes for a predictable outcome.

Table 4.19
Accused Officer(s)' Reaction

	Frequency	Percent
Says victim resisted arrest and refused to show identification	1	1.5
Suppresses facts or provides false information	2	3.1
Hires lawyer(s) to defend self	3	4.6
Pleads not guilty	2	3.1
Says victim threatened him or his family	3	4.6
Missing	54	83.1
TOTAL	65	100.0

Table 4.20
Police Department Public Relations and Resistance

	Frequency	Percent
Publishes figures on its ability to combat crime	1	1.5
Commissioner says officers need more training	1	1.5
Offers a settlement	1	1.5
Police official blames someone else for attack	1	1.5
Police official says victim resisted or was aggressive or dangerous	3	4.6
Missing	58	89.2
TOTAL	65	100.0

Percentages do not equal 100 due to rounding.

The Control Outcomes

Little can be said regarding the amount of public relations and resistance that the police department engages in when faced with charges of violence. Their responses are equally divided among publishing figures on their ability to combat crime; stating that officers need more training; offering a settlement with the victim(s); and blaming the victim(s) for instigating the incident by resisting arrest (see Table 4.20).

The most frequent internal control outcome for officers was suspension (12%), followed by charging the officer (8%) (see Table 4.21). However, when the entire police force was affected by a violence charge, the most frequent (6%) control initiative was a revision of rules, followed by the commissioner's proposal to revise the departmental procedures (see Table 4.22). Finally, in 2 percent of the cases, the commissioner made a recommendation to review the policy guidelines regarding the police

Table 4.21
Internal Control Outcomes Against Officer

	Frequency	Percent
Dismisses/fires officer	1	1.5
Launches internal investigation	2	3.1
Reassigns officer(s)	2	3.1
Suspends officer(s) without pay	3	4.6
Charges officer(s) with departmental charge	5	7.7
Suspends officer(s) from department	8	12.3
Missing	44	67.7
	-----	-----
TOTAL	65	100.0

Table 4.22
Internal Control Initiatives Against Entire Police Force

	Frequency	Percent
Issues policy statement	1	1.5
Commissioner recommends to committee to review guidelines	1	1.5
Implements new regulations	1	1.5
Increases staff of civilian complaints department	1	1.5
Commissioner proposes revision of rules	2	3.1
Revision of rules ordered	4	6.2
Missing/None	55	84.6
	-----	-----
TOTAL	65	100.0

Percentages do not equal 100 due to rounding.

practice in question (see Table 4.22). In general, these were very safe bureaucratic responses.

Finally, the most common (8%) external control initiative was a grand jury investigation, followed by a District Attorney investigation (6%) and a government-initiated inquest (5%). Most of the external control initiatives are government mandated (see Table 4.23).

SUMMARY

Given the amount of "missing data" and the consequent limited quantitative analysis feasible, the simplest inference to be made is that no attention or action followed the violent incident. However, the intensive case studies are more telling in terms of revealing the subtle patterns evident in the process of public police violence. As with the Toronto portion of this study, the shooting of Edmund Perry, the South Ozone

Table 4.23
External Control Intitiatives Against Police Force

	Frequency	Percent
One of a series of complaints that leads to an inquiry	1	1.5
Establishes official inquiry	1	1.5
Government asks third party to intervene	1	1.5
D.A. claims officers impeding probe	1	1.5
Coroner releases report	1	1.5
Commissioner turns down suspension	1	1.5
Police Commission launches inquiry	2	3.1
Government initiates inquest	3	4.6
D.A. investigates	4	6.2
Grand Jury investigates	5	7.7
Missing	45	69.2
TOTAL	65	100.0

Percentages do not equal 100 due to rounding.

Stun Gun incidents, and the Tompkins Square riots are analyzed in terms of the four-stage process model.

INTENSIVE CASE STUDIES

Deadly Force: The Shooting of Edmund Perry (June 13, 1985)[18]

On June 13, 1985, Lee Van Houten, a white New York City police officer on plainclothes duty, shot and killed Edmund E. Perry, a 17-year-old African-American man, on an Upper West Side street outside of Morningside Park. The circumstances of Perry's death were disputed by the police, witnesses, and the victim's family. The fact that Perry had recently graduated with honors from Philips Exeter Academy (New Hampshire) and the activism of the family's lawyer, C. Vernon Mason, attracted considerable attention to this case.

Media Initiation

The media reports of the shooting began immediately after the event took place and lasted almost daily for approximately two weeks. After that, reporting on the incident ceased for the next six months until the trial of Jonah Perry, Edmund's brother, who was implicated in the attack on Van Houten. High-profile, experienced *New York Times* reporters such as Myron Farber, Robert McFadden, and Selwyn Raab wrote most of the stories.

Arousal

Van Houten claimed that he opened fire after two youths, one of whom was Perry, jumped him from behind, knocked him down, and kicked and beat him in an apparent robbery attempt. Mason, an outspoken African-American civil rights lawyer, hired to represent the victim's family, said that the teenager had no criminal record and no reason to commit robbery.[19] Eventually, the police department, the victim's family, the family's clergy, and African-American residents of the Upper West Side became involved in the case.

Reaction

Reaction to this case was relatively extensive, involving the immediate family, their lawyers, the police officer involved, the coroner, and a vocal segment of the African-American community. Surprisingly, for some strange reason, little mention was made of the involvement of the Chief of Police. One day after the shooting, New York City Chief of Detectives Richard J. Nicastro announced at a news conference that the police had found witnesses who corroborated Van Houten's account that he was assaulted before shooting Perry. An autopsy on Perry's body was scheduled to be performed by Dr. Elliot M. Gross, the city's Chief Medical Examiner, but it was postponed until the family could get their own pathologist to attend. The result of the autopsy was somewhat predictable: Dr. Sidney B. Wienberg, retired Chief Medical Examiner of Suffolk County, representing the Perry family, contended that the shooting was unjustified and racially motivated.[20]

Funeral services in Harlem were attended by 1,000 to 1,500 people, including Perry's friends, neighbors, and fellow church members. Those in attendance—mostly African Americans—chanted "Stop Killing Us" and marched along the street holding candles that they received during the prayer service. Later, more than 400 people chanted, sang, and heard speeches outside of the 26th precinct police station in Harlem in protest of Perry's killing. The demonstrators called for Van Houten's prosecution and the appointment of a special prosecutor to look into what they suggested was part of a persistent pattern of police violence against African Americans by the NYPD.[21] This public display served to further attempts to mobilize the community to seek and subsequently obtain some form of justice.

Jonah Perry, Edmund's brother, a 19-year-old Cornell University sophomore, was later indicted and charged with joining in the attack on Van Houten. The charge against Jonah helped create increasing public doubt regarding the culpability of Van Houten. In the meantime, a grand jury determined that Van Houten had acted in self-defense. Veronica Perry, Edmund's and Jonah's mother, said that the grand jury had engaged in a cover-up. The situation garnered additional attention, because it provided an opportunity for the major characters involved to grandstand. For example, Robert M. Morgenthau, the Manhattan district attorney prosecuting the case, was running in a reelection against Vernon Mason for the same position. The situation was further exploited when Assemblyperson Herman Farrel questioned police department discipline, an action also interpreted as publicity seeking, as Farrel was running for the Democratic mayoral nomination.[22]

In the meantime, the Perry family hired Alton Maddox, another outspoken African-American lawyer, to defend Jonah against charges of assaulting and attempting to rob Van Houton. In court, Maddox suggested that, during the incident, Van Houton was drunk. The officer testified that he fired because he feared for his life. The trial dragged on for 13 days, and testimony in the case ended after the second prosecution witness, Desiree Solomon, implicated Jonah in the attack. When the opposing sides summed up in the Jonah Perry assault case, the defense charged, as others had done before, that it too was a cover-up.[23] Finally, the incident was the subject of a well-respected book, *Best Intentions: The Education and Killing of Edmund Perry*, by an award-winning author (Anson, 1975).

Outcomes

Although Jonah was acquitted, the issue over what actually ensued during the attack was never resolved. The incident was eventually heard in the New York State Supreme Court.[24] In 1989, approximately four years after the shooting and trial, the NYPD paid $75,000 to settle a $145 million wrongful-death suit launched by the Perry family. In their suit, the Perrys claimed that the officer was improperly trained and supervised and that the city had "permitted a pattern of illegal beatings and shootings of minority people."[25]

Torture: South Ozone Stun Gun Incidents (April 19, 1985)

During the spring of 1985, Mark Davidson, a white, 18-year-old high school student, told his lawyer that he was beaten and tortured with electric shocks by a police officer in the 106th precinct station house and was forced to make a false confession of taking $10 from an undercover officer in a marijuana sale.

Media Initiation

On April 20, 1985, Jimmy Breslin, a celebrated columnist and an author then with the *New York Post*, broke the first story of the South Ozone stun gun incident.[26] Anne Murray, a police reporter with the *Post*, who also covered the story, asserted that police at the precinct denied knowledge of the incident: "They probably hadn't read the paper," she commented. "Then everyone else [reporters] were kicked out. The integrity officer said that it was all trumped up. Little did we know but in the meantime, the Chief was being chewed out by the borough commander" about the incident.[27]

Arousal

Not only did reporters, the victim's lawyer, officers, borough commanders, and the Chief of Police get informed, but news of the incident reached high into the upper echelons of political power in New York City and New York State, including the district attorney and Mario Cuomo (then governor of New York State). Queens District Attorney John J. Santucci and the Police Department investigated the incident. The *New York Times* coverage by the same respected crime reporters who wrote about the Perry case lasted approximately two months. Press attention continued again almost a year later, during the trials of the officers accused of torturing Davidson. There were also sporadic articles throughout the following two years, as new victims came forward and the accused officers faced new trials.

Reaction

Santucci's office made a videotape of the youth's allegations and burnmarked body. Meanwhile, lockers and rooms at the police station were searched in an attempt to find evidence of wrongdoing.[28] Shortly thereafter, Everton K. Evelyn announced that he too was tortured and burned with an electric stun gun by Sergeant Richard A. Pike, the officer charged with abusing Davidson. Commissioner Ward also reported to the media that two new charges of brutality were being investigated, as well as all recent arrests by Pike's unit on street narcotics and by the entire 106th precinct. Subsequently, two more police officers were brought into custody; the entire top command of the 106th was ordered transferred, and the lieutenant in charge of guarding against brutality and corruption at the precinct was suspended without pay. Mayor Koch, feeling his credibility was at stake, asked U.S. Attorney General Edwin Meese III to open a separate inquiry into the charges. He was also quoted as saying that he would ask the city council to ban the sale and possession of electric stun guns.[29] Neither of these public relations gestures, however, had discernible effects.

In response to rising complaints of police brutality and allegations that some prisoners were tortured, Ward ordered the city's 327 top-ranking officers to a meeting. Perhaps in an attempt to win public relations kudos, he warned that "he would hold each personally responsible for brutality or corruption in their commands." Shortly after Ward's address, 19-year-old Robert Davis announced that he too was tortured with an electric stun gun at the 106th. In light of these revelations, Sydney Schanberg, a respected *New York Times* columnist, whose experiences in Cambodia were chronicled in the book and movie *The Killing Fields*, commented on the police brutality charges in New York City. He noted—in pro-police fashion—that, "Society asks police to work in coarse settings and then is shocked when these conditions inevitably harden officers." He further suggested that the community reach out to ease the frustration and alienation felt by many officers."[30]

In the wake of these allegations, Ward announced the abrupt retirement of Assistant Chief William F. Fitzpatrick, the top commander in Queens, and that brutality charges would henceforth be investigated by the Internal Affairs Bureau (IAB) rather than the CCRB. Assistant Chief Richard P. Dillon was named to replace Fitzpatrick, and Deputy Chief Dale F. Sullivan was given the IAB command with expanded powers. Next, Santucci reviewed all CCRB cases of police brutality in Queens County to determine if any others involved stun guns and broadened his inquiry into the alleged torture of suspects. In the meantime, the CCRB was the subject of a *New York Times* article that detailed charges by its critics dating back to its inception 19 years earlier. In particular, the story pointed out that the panel's independence had come under repeated questioning due to its composition of civilian employees of the Police Department. The article also suggested that stun guns were gaining popularity among law enforcement officials and civilians in New York and other cities because they were considered a benign and an effective method of self-defense. Koch and Deputy Police Commissioner Robert Goldman, however, expressed concern about purchases of the device by the public. Assemblyperson and mayoral aspirant Farrell, who was vocal in the Perry case, and City Council President Carol Bellamy both criticized Koch's handling of allegations of police brutality.[31] Farrell later announced the formation of a committee to promote a November referendum on establishing a new CCRB.

Afterwards, Santucci mentioned that some openings had developed in the "blue wall of silence built by police officers who had refused to cooperate with the inquiry into charges that suspects were tortured at the 106th." Consequently, he believed that he had sufficient evidence to seek indictments against four officers suspected of participating in, or tolerating, abuse of suspects to extract confessions to drug charges. The sudden retirement of Hamilton Robinson, commander of all uniformed officers in the NYPD, was also announced, along with those of three other commanders in Queens. Meanwhile, a fifth man, who claimed to have been tortured at the 106th, came forward. In response, during a news conference, Police Benevolent Association President Philip R. Caruso charged that Ward overreacted to allegations of torture. Nonetheless, five police officers from the 106th were eventually indicted on charges that prisoners in their custody were beaten and assaulted with electric stun guns. Lieutenant Steven Cheswick, Sergeant Richard Pike, and Officers Jeffrey Gilbert, Loren MacCarey, and Michael Aranda pleaded not guilty and were released without bail for a hearing on June 12, 1985.[32]

These incidents raised questions about overall police behavior and the effectiveness of police department programs to prevent misconduct, as did the fact that 6,698 complaints were filed in 1984 against city police officers for mistreatment and excessive force, about 600 more than in 1983. More damaging ammunition appeared in an op-ed article by NYCLU Staff Counsel Richard Emery, who suggested that the scandal at the 106th precinct was hardly an isolated incident of alleged police abuse. "The tragedy of the scandal," Emery said, is that it "has taken so long to focus public attention on reforms necessary to control police; and that the heart of the problem is the code of silence that binds police officers to protect wrongdoings of their partners."[33]

Meanwhile, community leaders in Ozone Park, New York City, assembled in front of the 106th in support of local police and against the "wholesale transfers" of several officers. Koch responded by appointing a nine-member advisory committee, led by John E. Zucott, to examine all aspects of the NYPD's management in light of the cases of alleged misconduct and brutality. Conterminously, Ward hoped to raise the standards of his officers by requiring psychological testing and some college education for all new recruits. The *New York Times* further suggested that Ward's uproar over the cases could be "transformed into a public mandate for long-term, in-depth, organizational changes including restoring the department's once-considerable discretion over appointments and promotions."[34]

Santucci later claimed that his investigation of stun-gun torture cases was being hampered by the unwillingness of police officers to come forward. He threatened to call police witnesses to testify before a federal rather than a state grand jury because of the more favorable immunity rules in that type of setting. Then Acting Justice John T. Gallagher dismissed conspiracy charges against the five Queens police officers, but he let other criminal charges stand. In the meantime, a criminal court judge in Queens said that Davidson was sufficiently punished for the alleged marijuana sale, and he dismissed the original drug possession charge.[35]

Pike and Gilbert went on trial on April 7, 1986, almost one year after being charged with assault and coercion against Davidson to confess to selling marijuana; three other officers faced later trials. The prosecution in the Pike and Gilbert case asserted that Davidson confessed to a minor drug charge in April 1985, only after Pike repeatedly shocked him with the gun and threatened to apply it to the youth's testicles. Lawyers for the defense told the jury that his clients did not inflict the injuries; burn marks on Davidson might have been made by a narcotics dealer and suggested that Davidson and one of his attorneys, Kornberg, would not be credible witnesses because they hoped to win a civil suit against the city. The prosecution's case appeared shaky at times; in particular, Davidson, under cross-examination, was unable to recall certain details of his arrest. Attempts to garner increased publicity were successful when a New York State Appeals Court overturned Justice Arthur J. Cooperman's order prohibiting lawyers and witnesses from talking to reporters about the trial.[36]

Gilbert, on trial in New York State Supreme Court, denied that he held down Davidson to allow Pike to torture the youth. Pike and Gilbert were eventually convicted of torturing Davidson and faced up to seven years in jail as well as trials in separate alleged incidents. Scenes from the Pike-Gilbert trial were continuously described in the dailies.[37]

Later, it was revealed that Nydia Becheiri, a juror in the trial, filed an affidavit charging that fellow jurors made her fearful of being physically abused if she did not agree with the guilty verdict. This prompted Pike's and Gilbert's defense attorneys to seek a new trial, but Cooperman upheld the conviction of the two. In July 1986, Pike and Gilbert were sentenced to two to six years in prison, while Cooperman denounced their actions.[38]

In January 1988, Pike, Gilbert, Cheswick, and MacCary went on trial in the second of four scheduled trials stemming from the stun gun tortures at the 106th precinct. Evelyn testified that Pike repeatedly tortured him with the stun gun, "delivering jolts of electricity that put him in agony and left him scarred." Gilbert, Cheswick, and MacCary, were accused of helping beat Evelyn. Cheswick, the highest-ranking officer to be charged with crimes stemming from the incident, denied that he had abetted the beating of Evelyn by other officers, and he asserted that the beating never took place.[39] Pike and MacCary were eventually convicted of felony assault and other charges for torturing Evelyn; Gilbert was found guilty of assaulting Evelyn; and Cheswick was convicted of official misconduct for abetting the beating. Justice Lawrence J. Finnegan Jr. of the New York State Supreme Court, Queens, sentenced MacCary to one-and-a-half years to four-and-a-half years in prison, Pike to two to six years, Gilbert to one-and-a-half years to four-and-a-half years, and Cheswick to three years' probation.[40] According to Ron Kuby, a well-known New York City civil rights lawyer, it was the "only time when justice was done."[41] In this incident, most of the charges against police officers were on a criminal, not a departmental, level. In the end, it resulted in four criminal trials and a number of officers going to jail.

Outcomes

Other than the abrupt retirements of police officials and an official investigation, external controls received more media attention. Shortly after the trials, New York State Senate Investigations Committee Chair Roy M. Goodman said that he would hold public hearings on the operation of the NYPD. Governor Cuomo's administration "impaneled" the Moreland Act Commission to examine accusations of brutality by police departments, not only in the city but around the state as well. U.S. Attorney Raymond J. Dearie then announced an investigation by federal prosecutors and the FBI of reports of torture and beatings at the 106th precinct.

Lawrence T. Kurlander, the governor's criminal justice coordinator, said that the commission would focus on "police recruitment, training, supervision, discipline and the usefulness of residency laws in connection with allegations of police brutality."[42] Former U.S. Attorney Paul J. Curran was appointed by Cuomo to head the commission; others on the panel were R. Harcourt Dodds, Flora Mancuso Edwards, Thomas F. Hastings, and Robert Hill Schwartz. The Moreland Committee dragged on for months before producing a document on police use of deadly force.[43]

Police Riot: Tompkins Square (August 6–7, 1988)[44]

Since the mid-1980s, gentrification of the Lower East Side of Manhattan (LES) had caused rents to skyrocket and "anarchists" to squat in abandoned buildings. Indeed, the most widely known quote in the LES was that "luxury housing is fast replacing affordable housing." Tompkins Square, with the biggest park in the neighborhood, became inhabited by homeless persons. Moreover, there was an increase in drug sales in the surrounding African-American and Latino neighborhood. A series of demonstrations—posited by some as representing a struggle for the rights of the homeless—was organized by a variety of grassroots organizations (e.g., RAGE-ON). The protesters comprised a collection of groups ranging from punk rockers, anarchists, and squatters to young professionals. Police later claimed that these groups rebuffed early efforts at negotiation and in some cases made clear that they were interested in confrontation.

The prelude occurred on July 30, when some members of the neighboring community (through the "right-wing" dominated Avenue A. Block Organization) wanted the police to enforce a 1:00 A.M. curfew on the park that had not been carried out previously.[45] The attempt to enforce the order was met with resistance by the "left-wing/progressive" members of the Block Organization, the Friends of Tompkins Square Park, Community Board #3, and neighborhood "malcontents." According to Kuby, "[G]roups of contentious and largely disorganized demonstrators clashed violently with inexperienced, undersupervised officers, who kicked and beat them, but [they] responded by hitting the cops. The cops got their asses kicked."[46]

On August 6–7, 1988, however, after viewing posters that threatened violence, the police decided to teach protestors a lesson. The result was a major confrontation between the police and members of the neighborhood, generally referred to as the Tompkins Square incident. Police officers, mainly from the 9th precinct, came to the Square in full force. Some of the demonstrators beat on car hoods, while others threw bottles, M-80s and M-100s, firecrackers that explode loudly. When the commander ordered the mounted police to charge the crowd, a number of bystanders inadvertently became involved in the fracas. Innocent people were struck with nightsticks and kicked on the ground, and "attempts [were] made by several officers to conceal their identity by covering or removing their shields" (Johnson report in note 44). This was the first riot in a number of years in which both the majority of victims and cops involved were Caucasian. The police riot—lasting four hours between the evening of August 6 and the early morning of August 7—resulted in 44 injuries (13 of which were police), 9 arrests, and nearly 100 complaints launched with the CCRB.

Media Initiation

The media, waiting on the sidelines for this confrontation, swiftly transmitted the event to the public, government, and police. Subsequently, the incident received national coverage. It was a dramatic news story, typified as a conflict between poor people, anarchists, communists, nihilists, rebels, and revolutionaries against the yuppie gentrifiers characterized by Tom Wolfe's book (later made into a film) Bonfire of the Vanities.[47]

Arousal

Initially, the police and the mayor's office either did not believe the reports or suggested that the protesters got their just deserts. In fact, during a press conference at City Hall the next day, Mayor Koch stated: "Take a cop on at your peril, and a cop at his peril will use undue force. We are prepared to support every cop who uses appropriate measures to prevent illegalities." Commissioner Ward said that he had no evidence that police acted wrongly, and Koch added that the police had no mandate "to be meek in the face of physical assault upon them."[48] Controversy over the incident was fueled by a four-hour long videotape made of the melee by Clayton Paterson, an "artist" occasionally preoccupied with supernatural rituals, living in the LES who made and sold hats for a living. The film served to increase the intrigue surrounding the event. As a result, members of the community, the NYCLU, the CCRB, radical lawyers, and the national artist community became involved.

Reaction

Investigations were made by the CCRB and the IAD. An official police investigation was conducted by Robert J. Johnston Jr., Chief of the Department. Complaints were received both at the CCRB and the NYCLU. The actors were primarily limited to the Chief of Police, the Center for Constitutional Rights, the NYCLU, and various journalists who wrote editorials. As a reaction to criticism of its handling of the park incidents, the NYPD quickly announced that it would step up training of recruits in controlling demonstrations. Further, some police experts suggested that experience and ad hoc improved response to protesters might prove more important than the actual training of recruits. Shortly after the riot, the police implemented a riot training session.[49] Two officers were charged with "wrongfully and without justification" striking two civilians during the riot. In the aftermath, authorities acquired Patterson's videotape. So commented Kuby, "We represented Clayton at one point in time. We regretted it. Clayton does a lot of self-promotion. He does videotaping and sells it to news stations." Kuby also stated that they (William Kunsler, his partner, another well-known, and now deceased, civil rights lawyer, and he) advised Patterson to turn over the tape to the police.[50] However, Paul Garring, one of the people who was beaten by police officers, also made a tape and "took a copy of this videotape to the offices of the U.S. Attorney for Southern District and Manhattan District Attorney and requested their assistance."[51] Several citizens also took photographs of the melee. In the meantime, Norman Siegel, executive director of the NYCLU, told everyone who was allegedly victimized to launch a complaint with the Center for Constitutional Rights (CCR).

In the wake of these complaints, Mayor Koch voiced his staunch support of Ward's handling of the incident. In response, Thomas Reppetto, president of the Citizens Crime Commission of New York City, in a *New York Times* op-ed piece, advanced the proposition that once appointed, police commissioners might have too much job security.

On August 11, Ward "conceded that the force had apparently blundered,"[52] and that a four-member panel of the CCRB would work with the full CCRB to investigate the incident. On August 23, the police held a press conference. The report, released at that event, pointed out that officers had engaged in serious misconduct and recommended better training for recruits.

The investigation into the Tompkins Square incident revealed many instances of conduct that appeared to violate either police rules or the law. Ward admitted that "poor planning and tactical errors led the police to lose control of the situation." The review of Patterson's videotape documented that the officers "did not wear badges, clubbed and kicked bystanders for no apparent reason and without arresting them, and streamed through the streets of the East Village in uncontrolled rage." A *New York Times* article asserted that the videotape of the protest in Tompkins Square was "just the latest example of civilians increasing their ability to document the behavior of and embarrass the city's police."[53]

The New York City Police Department's final report on violence in Tompkins Square suggested a breakdown in command and prescribed measures to ensure that it did not happen again. Ward stressed that "blame lay with commanded as well as those who largely failed to command." The commissioner "acknowledged that the roots of the melee also lie in the ... [basic] imbalance in today's police force." Although it is the "best educated and most intensively trained in memory, it is also the youngest and most inexperienced." This should come as no surprise, experts said; "48 percent of the force has less than five years' experience, one of the lowest levels of any department in the nation."[54]

Predictably, Caruso, during a press conference, defended the actions of the police involved in the clash, asserting that most of the brutality charges filed against officers would be invalidated. He also criticized the CCRB, calling its members a "bunch of incompetents." On the other hand, Siegel stressed that the follow-up of complaints by the CCRB was less than acceptable.[55] The police officers who were brought up on departmental charges were tried before an administrative law judge from the city's Office of Administrative Trials and Hearings rather than the Police Department's Deputy Commissioner of Trials, Rae-Downes Koshetz, or one of her assistant commissioners.[56]

The draft report by the CCRB concluded that only a small number of 115 complaints in the incident could be substantiated and officers positively identified. "Board members said that in other cases in which assertions of police abuse were established, many would not be pursued because officers were not identified positively." Board Chair Mary Burke Nicholas said that the "probe was hampered by difficulties in identifying individual officers and by refusal of all 400 officers and sergeants who were at the scene to volunteer evidence of wrong-doing." In the end, only two officers were charged with "wrongfully and without justification" striking two civilians.

Outcomes

A combination of public relations efforts and internal controls, both against individual officers and forcewide, was implemented. According to John Marzulli, a police reporter, "The police department now rotates cops on the front line [of a demonstration]. Because a cop can only take about 15 minutes of abuse."[57] According to the NYCLU,

fewer than a dozen officers have been found guilty of various offenses in departmental trial, with roughly a half-dozen cases still awaiting trial or decision. In only one of the cases that involved internal discipline by the Police department was the penalty more than 30 days suspension. . . . Of the six officers who were indicted and prosecuted by the Manhattan district attorney's office, none was convicted—either the charges were dismissed or the trials ended in acquittals. (NYCLU, 1990: 30)

Despite 120 cases launched with the CCRB, all were dismissed. Many civilians brought civil law suits against the police, and many received financial compensation. Reports ranged from all protesters having their charges dropped to five convictions of the demonstrators.

Chief Darcy retired after Ward severely criticized him for having "failed to properly supervise" the officers at the scene and to "take decisive action to control the situation." The precinct commander on the LES, Captain General F. McNamara, was subsequently relieved of his command. Deputy Inspector Joseph Wodarski was faulted for failing to take command and for two other lapses, and he was transferred from his post as commander of the Manhattan South Precinct. Siegel said that he found it "very hard to believe that if they [the NYPD] were using selective immunity, in the way that good prosecutors or lawyers know how to use it, that they would have come up empty handed."[58]

A *New York Times* editorial complained that "although the final report issued by the new CCRB recommended discipline for only a handful of officers, it indicted the whole department at the same time." It added that the NYPD "has a brutality problem as important as its corruption, a problem which must be eradicated aggressively to deter brutality and reassure the public." It is noteworthy but impossible to gauge how much this sequence of events affected the police action. Finally, Richard D. Emery, formerly associated with the NYCLU but at the time of the incident referred to by the media as a Manhattan civil rights lawyer who represented people injured by the police in demonstrations, said that the lack of charges against police officers was one of the most upsetting aspects of the clash. He added that, "the rarity of violent protests in recent years have also contributed to the problems in Tompkins Square. New York has one of the youngest police forces of any major city, and many of the officers on duty that night had little or no practical experience in facing such control problems."[59] Following these criticisms publicized in the media, the NYPD reported that it had revised crowd-control tactics in practice since the August 1988 melee. The revisions included doubling the number of sergeants and ranking officers overseeing less experienced officers, letting a demonstration run its course, and having dozens of officers in civilian clothes mingle in the crowd and quickly arrest people who hurled objects.[60] These practices were evident during a July 5, 1989, operation in which police helped city workers dismantle a shantytown erected in Tompkins Square. The park had been closed since June 3. According to Michael Farrin, a community activist and freelance editor who lived directly across from the park and was present the night of the melee, there was official division in the community; the community board had voted against closing the park.[61]

Today, according to individuals who live and work in the LES, the police who monitor the Square and the LES have become more adept at hiding brutality. For example, more plainclothes police are working in the community. Now, when people are arrested, they are immediately surrounded by officers to shield them from the press and onlookers. Furthermore, people are "busted on trumped-up charges." As a response, activists now carry their passports, so if they are arrested, they will have proper identification and will avoid being taken into custody. Otherwise, demonstrators are arrested and left to wait in jail before proper identification is made.[62] Consequently, the LES has resembled a police state such as Belfast or the Occupied Territories. Police are routinely seen on the roofs of many buildings, and much to the consternation of citizens, they even hang out on the stairs of apartment buildings in the neighborhood. Their presence, especially because of the portable radios they carry, disturbs many of the individuals who live there. In response to complaints, the police claim that they are simply patrolling the area, sometimes in search of people who have thrown bottles at them.

SUMMARY

In the aftermath of these incidents, there were dismissals and transfers of police officers and administrators and the dropping of charges. Many of the alleged victims filed civil suits and were able to collect some monetary compensation. And in some neighborhoods, there was an increase in police presence. Consolidating both the quantitative and qualitative findings over the period examined, the greatest changes in the police force that resulted as direct consequences of these three incidents were forced early retirement, transfers, retraining, and the laying of criminal charges against individual police officers, but with no appreciable changes made forcewide. The NYPD also explored the use of new, less-than-lethal force equipment and greater controls on the use of already existing weapons. Although resistance was not detectable, public relations and controls—both internal and external—were implemented following each case. Regardless, the public relations efforts of the NYPD seem to be a dominant response to accusations of police use of excessive force.

The violence continues. Despite efforts to reform the department—particularly through the hiring of Lee Brown in 1990,[63] who during that time was perceived to be one of the most progressive chiefs in the United States and had the endorsement of the PBA, the expansion of community policing (McElroy, Cosgrove, and Sadd, 1993) and the introduction of CompStat, a management philosophy and practice that holds precinct and borough commanders accountable for crime rates in their jurisdiction—the NYPD continues to suffer periodic outbreaks of celebrated incidents of police violence, which was the subject of a 1996 report by Amnesty International on "Police Brutality and Excessive Force" in the City (Amnesty International, 1996). In the latter part of the 1990s, the NYPD was forced, once again, to confront allegations of police violence in connection with the 1997 arrest of Abner Louima and the 1998 shooting of Amadou Diallo.

NOTES

1. According to Astor (1971: 4), "History's effect cannot be underestimated, for past performance and tradition influence much of the quality of police work today." The history of the force can be divided according to the periods commanded by its successive commissioners (e.g., Patrick V. Murphy, Donald Cawley, Benjamin Ward, and Lee Brown) or mayors (e.g., Robert F. Wagner, John Lindsey, Ed Koch, and David Dinkins). Each new commissioner and mayor exerted subtle changes in the structure of their municipal administrations including the police. Alternatively, the Knapp Commission hearing in, 1971 left such an indelible scar on the police department that many reporters and police officers divide the force's contemporary history into pre-Knapp and post-Knapp (see Reuss-Ianni (1984: 3) for a similar perception). These time frames can be used as a heuristic device, but it will not be employed in such a manner here.

2. The NYPD has been the setting for many fictionalized books, films, and television series that have created a number of stereotypes and caricatures of the city's police officers, criminals, and victims (Radano, 1968; Maas, 1973; Adcock, 1984; McAlary, 1987). Additionally, a considerable amount of academic research has been conducted on the department (e.g., Bopp, 1971; Rogowski et al., 1971; Kahn, 1975; Meyer, 1976; Rosen, 1981). Access to primary source material and key decision makers in the force is difficult. Official documents are inconvenient to access for those not living in the immediate area. For example, the NYPD restricts the dissemination of its annual report. Moreover, requests for official access to members of the force must go through the organization's Department of Public Information. Finally, neighborhoods differ so much in New York City that it is difficult to make generalizations about policing the city as a whole.

3. "The complete transition from the constable-watch system to the uniformed police took . . . a decade in New York, 1843–53" (Monkkonen, 1981: 42).

4. For a detailed review of this incident, see Barnes (1983).

5. For a detailed review of this incident, see Shapiro and Sullivan (1964).

6. *The Negro in Harlem* (1935: 65), unpublished report, as quoted in Stark (1972).

7. United States (1947).

8. United States (1967).

9. One persisting characteristic of the NYPD is that it is a huge bureaucracy that is slow to change (Niederhoffer, 1969, ch. 1). There are numerous layers of decision making, and political considerations must be taken into account when any changes are proposed and implemented. Perhaps the starkest example of

difficulties with reforming the NYPD is illustrated by Reuss-Ianni (1984: ch. 6). She discusses the problems connected with implementing the 1977 management-by-objectives plan, first at headquarters and then at the local precincts. The project was doomed from the beginning; it did not apply to policing, and the differences between the "two cultures of policing" (management versus street cops) were too great for it to have an effect.

10. For a more in-depth discussion of these controls, see Daley (1972); Alex (1976: 69); Murphy (1977: 177); Reuss-Ianni (1984); Bennett (1989); and Tobin (1991).

11. For a review of these offices, see for example, Viteritti, (1973: 24); Murphy (1977: 155); Reuss-Ianni (1984: 104); Liman and Gitter et al. (1985: 8); Baden (1989: 54); and NYCLU (1990).

12. For a more in-depth coverage of these controls see, for example, Levi (1977: 27); Gammage and Sachs (1972).

13. In other words, after a while, the public loses interest in issues.

14. For the history of governing New York City, see, for example, Sayre and Kaufman (1965); Glazer and Moynihan (1970); Newfield and Barret (1988).

15. The reaction variables of national police organizations and businesses and their associations were dropped because all information was missing.

16. For an in-depth review of the coroner's report of these cases, see Liman and Gitter et al. (1985).

17. In sum, the Perry, South Ozone, and Tompkins Square incidents were selected for intensive review. However, none of these events can be analyzed in isolation from each other. For example, the Conyers Commission Investigation (United States, 1984), which lasted for four years, may well have set a precedent for future governmental and public responses and consequently dampened the need or desire to endure another large-scale inquiry.

18. Some people interviewed suggested that it was a bad case because it was a clean shoot (i.e., it was legal). The reader should be reminded that the purpose of case selection is not to examine cases where the police have been found guilty but rather those that attracted considerable media attention. For an interesting review of Perry's background, see Anson (1975).

19. Leonard Buder, "Honor Student, 17, Is Killed by Policeman on West Side," *New York Times*, June 14, I, 1: 1, 1985.

20. Leonard Buder, "Police Say Others Saw Student Attack Officer," *New York Times*, June 15, I, 1: 4, 1985; William R. Greer, "Search for Man Goes on in Attack on Officer," *New York Times*, June 16, I, 26: 4, 1985; Peter Kerr, "Student Died of Stomach Wound," *New York Times*, June 17, II, 3: 5, 1985. Gross' office was subject to public investigation in 1985 for allegedly "obstructing investigations and prosecution of cases, and falsifying or obstructing autopsy reports or death certificates." See, for example, Liman and Gitter et al. (1985: 2) for the inquiry's findings.

21. Myron A. Farber, "Slain Student Is Eulogized at Memorial," *New York Times*, June 19, II, 7: 1, 1985; Susan Heller Anderson and David W. Dunlop, "New York Day by Day," *New York Times*, June 20, II, 3: 4, 1985; Peter Kerr, "X of Youth's Killing," *New York Times*, June 22, I, 33: 1, 1985.

22. Marcia Chambers, "Brother of Slain Student Indicted," *New York Times*, July 4, I, 1: 5, 1985.

23. M. A. Farber, "A Shattering of Destinies," *New York Times*, July 4, I, 1: 6, 1985; Robert D. McFadden, "Farrell Accuses Mayor of Triggering Violence," *New York Times*, July 8, II, 3: 5, 1985. M. A. Farber, "Brother of Honors Student from Harlem Goes on Trial," *New York Times*, January 10, II, 3: 5, 1986; M. A. Farber, "Officers Tells of Shooting Honors Student to Death," *New York Times*, January 14, II, 3: 3, 1986; M. A. Farber, "Testimony Ends in Assault Trial of Jonah Perry," *New York Times*, January 17, II, 3: 1, 1986; M. A. Farber, "Last Argument Offered in Trial of Jonah Perry," *New York Times*, January 22, II, 3: 4, 1986.

24. M. A. Farber, "Jonah Perry Acquitted of Mugging Officer Who Fatally Shot Brother," *New York Times*, January 23, I, 1: 4, 1986; M. A. Farber, "For Many Jurors, Little Was Proved in Perry Case," *New York Times*, January 26, I, 21: 1, 1986.

25. Robert D. McFadden, "Settlement Reached in Perry Wrongful-Death Suit," *New York Times*, May 13, I, 29: 3, 1989. According to New York City activist lawyer Stanley Cohen, "If you throw six figures at a poor black family they will take it. It's also a number of years after the controversy has taken place. And they routinely have a nondisclosure rider."

26. Breslin is a good friend of Kornburg, the defendant's lawyer, and it is probable that this is how he found out about the incident. Breslin has since gone to *Newsday*.

27. Based on a personal interview with the author, July 21, 1990.

28. Robert D. McFadden, "Youth's Charges of Torture by an Officer Spurs Inquiry," *New York Times*, April 22, II, 3: 5, 1985.

29. Selwyn Raab, "2 More Officers Charged in Inquiry into Torture at Queen's Precinct," *New York Times*, April 24, II, 3: 5, 1985, *New York Times*, April 25, I, 1: 2, 1985.

30. Selwyn Raab, "Ward Calls Top New York Officers to a Meeting on Brutality Charges," *New York Times*, April 26, I, 1: 1, 1985; William R. Greer, "Turmoil in Troubled Precinct Centers on 'the Strip'," *New York Times*, April 26, II, 1: 1, 1985; Selwyn Raab, "Ward Tells Top N-Y Officers They Will Be Liable in Brutalities," *New York Times*, April 27, I, 1: 2, 1985.

31. Sydney H. Schanberg, "Thoughts about Police Scandals," *New York Times*, April 27, I, 23: 6, 1985; Selwyn Raab, "Stricter Inquiries in Brutality Cases Pledged by Ward," *New York Times*, April 28, I, 1: 6, 1985; Robert D. McFadden, "Brutality Inquiry Widened in Queens," *New York Times*, April 28, I, 34: 1, 1985; "Review Board Has Had Critics Since its Start," *New York Times*, April 28, II, 34: 1, 1985; and "Defensive Use of Stun Guns Increases," *New York Times*, April 28, I, 43: 4, 1985.

32. Josh Barbanel, "Farrell and Bellamy, at a Forum Criticize Mayor," *New York Times*, April 29, II, 3: 1, 1985; "Santucci Says Some Officers Are Aiding Torture Inquiry," *New York Times*, April 29, II, 3: 5, 1985; Robert McFadden, "No. 3 on Police Force Retiring Amid Torture Case, *New York Times*, April 30, II, 1: 4, 1985; Josh Barbanel, "P.B.A. Faulting Ward's Actions in Torture Case," *New York Times*, May 1, II, 8: 1, 1985.

33. "5 Police Officers Indicted By Jury in Torture Case," *New York Times*, May 3, I, 1: 2, 1985; Frank Lynn, "Farrell, Switching Position, Seeks Jackson's Help," *New York Times*, May 3, II, 4: 2, 1985; Jane Perley, "Ward Tries to Patch Up His Chain of Command," *New York Times*, May 5, IV, 8: 1, 1985; Jane Perley and

Selwyn Raab, "Rising Brutality Complaints Raise Questions about New York Police," *New York Times*, May 6, I, 1: 3, 1985, continued II, 5:1.

34. Richard Emery, "Curbing New York's Police," *New York Times*, May 7, I, 31: 1, 1985; U.P.I., *New York Times*, "Ozone Park Rally Backs Officers," May 7, II, 24: 3, 1985; Joyce Purnick, "Koch Names Panel to Recommend New Procedure at Police Department," *New York Times*, May 8, II, 3: 3, 1985.

35. Sam Roberts, "Police at Cross Roads: A Choice to Turn Rising Adversity into Advantage," *New York Times*, May 9, II, 1: 1, 1985; "Santucci Weighs Shift in Inquiry on Torture," *New York Times*, May 13, II, 6: 4, 1985; *New York Times*, June 26, II, 3: 3, 1985. *New York Times*, May 13, 26, II, 3: 3, 1985; AP, "1 Count Dismissed in Stun-Gun Case,"

36. Joseph P. Fried, "Dismissal for Stun Gun Accuser," *New York Times*, June 27, II, 3: 1, 1985; Joseph P. Fried, "Trial Begins Today for Policemen Accused of Using Stun Gun on Prisoners in Queens," *New York Times*, April 7, II, 3: 2, 1986; Joseph P. Fried, "Stun Gun Used on Youth, Jury Is Told," *New York Times*, April 12, I, 29: 5, 1986; Joseph P. Fried, "Student Tells Jury 2 Officers Burned Him with Stun Gun," *New York Times*, April 19, I, 30: 1, 1986; Joseph P. Fried, "Stun-Gun Accuser Fails to Recall Details of Arrest," *New York Times*, April 22, II, 3: 2, 1986.

37. Leonard Buder, "Ruling Upsets Order to Limit Trial Publicity," *New York Times*, April 23, II, 3: 1, 1986; Joseph P. Fried, "Officer in Stun-Gun Trial Denies That He Aided in Assault," *New York Times*, April 30, II, 3: 1, 1986; Joseph P. Fried, "Lawyers Clash on Evidence in Officers Stun Gun Trial," *New York Times*, May 1, II, 2: 5, 1986; Joseph P. Fried, "Two Queens Officers Convicted in Stun Gun Trial," *New York Times*, May 3, I, 1: 4, 1986.

38. Joseph P. Fried, "Reporters Notebook: Scenes at Stun Gun Trial," *New York Times*, May 4, I, 42: 3, 1986; Joseph P. Fried, "Juror Contends Peers Pressured Stun Gun Vote," *New York Times*, June 7, I, 31: 6, 1986; Anonymous, "Verdict Is Upheld in Stun-Gun Case," *New York Times*, July 15, II, 4: 3, 1986.

39. Joseph P. Fried, "Ex Officer Gets 2 to 6 Years in Queens Stun Gun Torture," *New York Times*, July 18, II, 3: 5, 1986; Anonymous, "WEAPONRY," *New York Times*, November 4, II, 1: 1, 1986; AP, "Figure in '85 Stun Gun Case Seized After Brawl With wife," *New York Times*, October 18, I, 42: 5, 1987; Joseph P. Fried, "4 Former and Suspended Officers Are Accused in 2nd Stun Gun Trial," *New York Times*, January 10, I, 29: 1, 1988; M. A. Farber, "For Many Jurors, Little Was Proved in Perry Case," *New York Times*, January 26, II, 3: 1, 1988.

40. Stacey Okun, "Queens Police Are Accused of Torture," *New York Times*, February 2, II, 2: 3, 1988; Joseph P. Fried, "Suspended Policeman Denies Role in Beating of Marijuana Dealer," *New York Times*, February 18, II, 5: 5, 1988.

41. Based on a personal interview with the author, July 7, 1990.

42. Joseph P. Fried, "Stun Gun-Trial Ends With Four Being Convicted," *New York Times*, February 25, II, 2–6, 1988; Joseph P. Fried, "Judge Assails 4 Ex-Policemen in Sentencing in Queens Torture Case," *New York Times*, March 30, II, 3: 1, 1988.

43. Edward A. Gargan, "A State Hearing Set on Actions by City's Police," *New York Times*, May 16, I, 1: 5, 1985; Anonymous, "Moreland Act Dates Back to 1907," *New York Times*, May 21, II, 2: 2, 1985; Edward A. Gargan, "Cuomo to Order Review of Police across the State," *New York Times*, May 21, I, 1: 2, 1985; Jeffrey Schmaltz, "Governor Picks Panel to Review Police Brutality," *New York*

Times, June 6, II, 11: 3, 1985; Selwyn Raab, "Goodman Assails Police on Recruit Screenings," *New York Times*, September 24, II, 3: 5, 1985; Josh Barbanel, "New Police Goals in Crowd Control," *New York Times*, August 13, I, 1: 1, 1985.

44. For a review of the situation, see Memo: From Robert J. Johnston Jr. Chief of Department to Police Commissioner re: Tompkins Square Park Incident, August 23, 1988. Also see letter from Norman Siegel, executive director, NYCLU, to Sandra Marsh, August 10, 1989, and NYCLU (1990). Police-community friction in the LES has a long legacy. In the late 1960s, the Black Panther Party assassinated police in the Lower East Side. Residents applauded when these events took place.

45. The problems with Tompkins Square have a long history, often framed in terms of whether the city can legislate what happens in the park.

46. Based on a personal interview with the author, July 21, 1990.

47. Referring in this case to the celebrated novel by Tom Wolfe.

48. *New York Newsday*, August 9, 1988, p. 25.

49. Richard Levine, "Koch's Verdict: Ward Is Not guilty," *New York Times*, August 13, I, 30: 1, 1988.

50. See also letter to the editor, *The Shadow*, Issue #6, September 1989, p. 19.

51. The NYCLU produced a document (1990) that served as an unofficial inquiry into the incident and made a series of recommendations.

52. *New York Newsday*, August 11, 1988, p. 3.

53. Todd S. Purdum, "Melee in Tompkins Sq. Park: Violence and Its Provocation," *New York Times*, August 14, I, 1: 4, 1988.

54. Constance L. Hays, "Home Videos Turn Lenses on the Police," *New York Times*, August 15, II, 1: 2, 1988.

55. NYCLU, "Tompkins Square Park: The First 100 Days, November 19, 1988; David E. Pitt, "Roots of Tompkins Sq. Clash Seen in Young and Inexperienced Officer," *New York Times*, August 25, II, 7: 1, 1988.

56. Constance L. Hays, "Union Leader Backs Police in Tompkins Sq. Clash," *New York Times*, August 27, I, 29: 1, 1988.

57. Based on a personal interview with the author, July 9, 1990.

58. David E. Pitt, "Few Officers Face Charges in Park Melee," *New York Times*, March 22, II, 1: 5, 1989.

59. "Not the Last Word on Tompkins Square," *New York Times*, April 22, I, 26: 1, 1989.

60. Based on a personal interview with the author, August 30, 1991.

61. Interviewed on August 28, 1991.

62. James C. McKinley, Jr., "New Tactics with Cooling Park Protests," *New York Times*, July 29, I, 27: 5, 1989; Todd S. Purdum, "When Police and Protesters Break an Unwritten Code," *New York Times*, August 21, 1988, p. E6.

63. James C. McKinley, Jr., "What Will It Take to Make Foot Patrol an Enticing Career," *New York Times*, October 7, 1990.

Chapter 5

Beyond Apathy

Although the various responses to acts of police violence that took place in the two cities seem diverse, a number of empirically derived generalizations can be made from their analysis. This book concludes with the results from the statistical tests performed on selected hypotheses of the model. Also, the similarities and differences between the two sets of qualitatively generated cases (i.e., the police use of deadly force, torture, and police riot situations) for Toronto and New York City, respectively, are analyzed. Finally, the implications of these results are discussed.

RESULTS FROM QUANTITATIVE ANALYSIS

Despite the limited utility of media reports as a source of information to determine much beyond the act of police violence, a number of hypotheses can be tested.

Comparison of Missing Information

The data for each city individually (Toronto, 51 cases, and New York City, 65 cases) and for both cities combined (n = 116) were analyzed (see Appendix E). With the exception of "number of people/organizations who got involved after the incident," and "time elapsed between first and last incident," 34 out of the 36 variables coded had missing information. Most likely, this finding reflects reporters' and editors' decisions that the item was not important or not available for inclusion.

Several questions emerge from the missing data, particularly as it re-

Table 5.1
Chi-Square Tests of Toronto Data[a]

Degree of Arousal and Episodic Variables

Variable	d.f.	Chi-Square obtained	Chi-Square critical
NUOFVICT	4	2.72	9.49
PUBLICFI	2	2.17	5.99
SEVERITY	8	9.28	15.51
GENVIC	2	1.44	5.99
ACTIVITY	4	1.46	9.49
DEMEANOR	2	2.40	5.99
AGEOFPOL	6	8.00	12.59
AGEOFVIC	22	28.00	33.92
NUMOFVIC	4	3.62	9.49
NUMOFPOL	10	8.16	18.31
RACEOFVIC	2	3.04	5.99
MORAL	2	2.45	5.99
PERCEPTN	2	6.86	5.99
SCOPE	16	31.04	26.30
ELAPSED	62	102.00	79.08

a. Degree of arousal is measured by number of articles, categorized into low, medium, and high, where statistics can be computed (i.e., statistics cannot be computed when number of non-empty rows or columns is 1).

lates to police departments. For example, do law enforcement agencies implement changes without informing the public? Yes, but would it not be in their best interests for damage control—or, more generally, public relations purposes—to publicize changes made in response to acts of police violence? Alternatively, do police departments enact policies to avoid focusing citizen attention on excessive police violence, as this might be seen as an admission of culpability? No definitive answers can be found to these questions. Furthermore, the missing information could also reflect a paucity of detail that single newspaper sources provide, the shortness of the time covered, problems with the case selection criteria, or improper or insensitive scaling techniques.[1]

Chi-Square Tests

As previously stated, most events produced only one newspaper article and only one to three people (e.g., police, politicians, activists) responded to the incident. Two chi-square analyses were performed on the episode variables.

Relationships among the episode variables and degree of arousal in the Toronto sample were tested with chi-square analysis. Only chi-square values for three variables—"perception," "scope," and "time elapsed"—were significant at the alpha = .05 level (see Table 5.1), hence the null hypothesis of no relationship was rejected on these variables. As with

Table 5.2
Chi-Square Statistics for New York City Data[a]

Degree of Arousal and Episodic Variables

Variable	d.f.	Chi-Square obtained	Chi-Square critical
SEVERITY	8	7.33	15.51
NUOFVICT	6	13.76	12.59*
PUBLICFI	2	3.51	5.99
GENVIC	4	7.68	9.49
GENOFPOL	2	.65	5.99
ACTIVITY	4	4.30	9.49
DEMEANOR	2	.47	5.99
AGEOFVIC	18	19.50	28.87
NUMOFVIC	6	9.53	12.59
NUMOFPOL	10	6.61	18.31
RACEOFVIC	2	2.35	5.99
RACEOPOL	4	2.18	5.99
PERCEPTN	4	2.49	9.49
SCOPE	10	20.23	18.31*
ELAPSED	44	108.76	55.76*

a. Degree of arousal is measured by number of articles, categorized into low, medium, and high, where statistics can be computed (i.e., statistics cannot be computed when number of non-empty rows or columns is 1).
1-tailed Signif: *—.01.

the previous test, there could be a significant relationship with the non-significant variables if they were categorized, however, none of these factors have many values beyond the ones that currently exist.

In the New York City sample, factors specified in the model about what should influence arousal (i.e., the episode characteristics) were cross-tabbed with the "degree of arousal" (i.e., the number of articles printed), which was categorized into low, medium, and high.[2]

To establish whether there was a relationship among the episode variables and degree of arousal, chi-square analyses were performed. For the New York City data, chi-square tests on episode characteristics and degree of arousal produced some chi-square values significant at the alpha = .05 level. The obtained chi-squares for "number of victims," "scope," and "time elapsed" exceed the critical value of chi-square at alpha = .05 (see Table 5.2), hence the null hypothesis that there is no relationship between these episode characteristics and degree of arousal is rejected. Even though there could be a significant relationship among the nonsignificant variables if they were categorized, none of these variables have many values beyond the ones that currently exist.

Generalizing between the two samples, the most consistent findings were that there was a relationship between "scope" and "time elapsed between first and last article."

Table 5.3
Correlations between High Arousal (as measured by moderate and high
number of articles) and Other Variables from the Toronto Data Set at Each
Stage of the Model[a]

Moderate and High Degree of Arousal and Episode Characteristics

Variable	Cases	Correlation
DEMEANOR	4	.98*
ACTIVITY	17	.49
AGEOFPOL	3	.50

Moderate and High Degree of Arousal and Reaction Variables

Variable	Cases	Correlation
SCOPE	29	.81**
ELECTED	3	-.50
MEDIA	3	.69
ELAPSED	30	.50**

```
NUOFVICT = Number of victims involved in incident
DEMEANOR = Demeanor of victims
SCOPE    = Number of actors that got involved after the
           incident
UNION    = Police union/association reaction
VICTIMS  = Victim or victim's family's reaction
ELAPSED  = Time elapsed between first and last article
ACTIVITY = Activity level of victim(s)
AGEOFPOL = Age of police officer(s)
ELECTED  = Elected politicians' reactions
MEDIA    = Media reactions
```

N of cases: 30   1-tailed Signif: * - .01   ** - .001

a. Only those correlations above .49, regardless of directionality, are reported.

Correlational Analysis

Correlations were run between all variables for those cases for which
there is demonstrable arousal (i.e., moderate or high), measured by the
variable "number of articles" for the two data sets, but rejecting those
cases with only one article.[3] Regardless of the data set analyzed, few of
the variables produced significant correlations, and none of the outcomes
factors resulted in significant correlations. In the Toronto case, "demeanor of victim(s)," "activity level of victim," "age of victim," "scope,"
"media reactions," and time elapsed" were positively correlated at the
alpha =.01 significance level (see Table 5.3). "Elected officials' reactions,"
and "number of articles" were negatively correlated. For the New York
City data, "number of victims," "demeanor of victim(s)," "scope," "union activity," "victim(s) activity," and "time elapsed" were positively

Table 5.4
Correlations between High Arousal (as measured by moderate and high
number of articles) and Other Variables from the New York City Data Set at
Each Stage of the Model[a]

Moderate and High Degree of Arousal and Episode Characteristics

Variable	Cases	Correlation
NUOFVICT	25	.72**
DEMEANOR	4	.66

Moderate and High Degree of Arousal and Reaction Variables

Variable	Cases	Correlation
SCOPE	23	.94**
UNION	3	.79
VICTIMS	7	.57
ELAPSED	26	.80**

```
NUOFVICT = Number of victims involved in incident
DEMEANOR = Demeanor of victims
SCOPE    = Number of actors that got involved after the
           incident
UNION    = Police union/association reaction
VICTIMS  = Victim or victim's family's reaction
ELAPSED  = Time elapsed between first and last article
```

N of cases: 26   1-tailed Signif: * - .01 ** - .001

a. Only those correlations above .49, regardless of directionality, are reported.

correlated at the alpha =.01 level (see Table 5.4). Generalizing between
the two samples, the most consistent findings were that the worse the
"demeanor of the victim(s)," the greater the "scope," and the greater the
"time elapsed between first and last article," the higher the arousal.

Summary of Quantitative Analysis

Taking the quantitative results at face value, there is little police, community, or governmental reaction to the majority of police violence identified in this investigation. On the other hand, there is one important
similarity between the two cities: the "number of actors that get involved" and the "time elapsed between the first and last article" are
significant. Few of the other variables specified in the model are significant. As predicted, perhaps there are more subtle factors that are not
amenable to this type of quantitative analysis. Before examining alternate
explanations, the results from the qualitative portion of the study are
discussed.

RESULTS FROM QUALITATIVE ANALYSIS: CASE STUDY COMPARISONS

Introduction

As expected, quantitative analysis may have obscured individual differences and may not be sensitive enough to analyze the more subtle processes that follow in the wake of police use of excessive force. Consequently, the six different cases of police violence were analyzed in detail. Similar types of deadly force, torture, and police riot incidents that fit the public police violence context were selected from each city. By analyzing and comparing them (e.g., Evans and Perry, Turner and South Ozone Stun Gun, Morrish Road and Tompkins Square), similarities and/or differences in the way these types of events were reacted to by the community, government, and police of these two cities were determined. It must be understood that most of the incidents selected for intensive investigation are in fact anomalies in the sense that they, unlike the norm, generated more than one story or media report and some type of publicized public, government, and police reaction.

Deadly Force: Evans versus Perry

In both the Evans and Perry incidents of police use of deadly force, a coroner's inquest was the immediate response by the criminal justice system. To enhance the legitimacy of the officers' actions, the police lawyers, during the coroner's hearings and trials, tried to use the real or alleged victim's past criminal record, emphasized the criminal nature of the event, or stressed the fact that officers who were accused of the shootings also required hospitalization to deflect attention away from the policeman's behavior and onto the victim's. On the other hand, the victim's lawyers tried to capitalize on the racial nature of the shootings (i.e., white officer shooting an African-American/black suspect). Although the public (primarily black/African-American) responded with mass demonstrations against the police actions, no reported changes in policy and procedure were announced or discovered through my investigations of the respective police departments. If no convictions resulted, the police forces were under no legal or other relevant obligation to implement change. The lack of convictions meant that, in their eyes, they were "clean," and this outcome probably motivated the police's resistance to admission of culpability and unwillingness to recommend any changes to ameliorate similar situations in the future. Despite the lack of formal sanctions applied to either the police officers or departments, there was, however, an out-of-court settlement to the Evans and Perry families several years later as a result of civil suits filed by the plaintiffs.

Torture: Turner versus South Ozone

In the Toronto alleged torture situation, the officers accused of hurting the victim (i.e., Turner) were criminally charged but not convicted. Logically, no senior officers were disciplined, and despite a brief video camera experiment, no policies and practices were changed. In the New York City counterpart case, on the other hand, not only were officers either suspended or transferred, but the four individuals responsible for the action were convicted and incarcerated.

Moreover, some "distinguished" NYPD police brass saw their careers prematurely end because of their failure to supervise their subordinates as a consequence of the original incident. The Toronto community offered neither criticism nor support of the police during the Turner case, whereas in the South Ozone incidents, many New Yorkers of the local community mobilized behind the police. In the latter incident, however, the citizens' response could not outweigh the evidence of police wrongdoing revealed in court, and the officers in question were punished. In both events, however, police responses were initiated by their internal control mechanisms (i.e., internal affairs departments) but directed primarily at particular officers or members of a team or precinct rather than the whole force. These internally driven responses were effective in appeasing an upset public or in repairing the community's tarnished image of its police. What was less publicly known is that the police brass who acted on their own initiative to temporarily appease the community were, at the same time, also preempting external control initiatives.

Police Riot: Morrish Road versus Tompkins Square

In both the Morrish Road and Tompkins Square police riots, witnesses had incontrovertible evidence of official wrongdoing, namely, videotapes of the respective incidents. As with the 1991 videotape of Los Angeles Police Department (LAPD) officers beating Rodney King, this type of evidence should be most damaging to police and thus should become the most important, effective motivation for change in police policy and practices directed against the entire force. In the events under analysis here, the police's initial internal response was to request or subpoena the tapes from the persons or organizations who recorded the incident. Subsequently, proposals and initiatives for better training of officers, both those who participated in the action and those currently in the police academy, were articulated to the media, perhaps in an effort at damage control before the release of any official internal reports. Moreover, such announcements neglected to mention the type of punishment meted out to the officers involved in the police riot incidents. Eventually, the police either announced the demotion of senior officers or changes in the com-

mand structure (New York City only) or apologized to the victims (Toronto only). In both cases, the police and third-party complaint systems
(i.e., CIRPA, OPCC, and CCRB) received numerous depositions, mainly
from victims and occasionally from outraged members of the public.
Additionally, the respective Chiefs of Police launched an extensive public
relations campaign to ensure the community that their concerns were
being addressed and that in the future such incidents would be prevented and avoided at all cost.

Summary of Qualitative Comparative Results

In general, we can probably say that the actors who get aroused and
their reactions and outcomes are similar for each type of police violence.
There is greater homogeneity among reactions to particular types of police use of excessive force than among different kinds of police violence.

With respect to media initiation, in both cities no general consensus
can be drawn. In some cases, one reporter covered the incident, while in
others, successive reporters took over the stories. Interest was sustained
at different times because of the news value of the developments in the
story, ranging from the initial incident to community mobilization to
trial.

During the arousal stage, similar agencies in both cities became involved. Although there was no similar institution to CIRPA in New York
City, complaints were launched with the CCRB. Use of these agencies,
however, was made primarily as a strategic ploy by plaintiffs, because
their lawyers encouraged them to do so. The differences in response
cannot be accounted for nationally or culturally (Canada versus the
United States). In all cases of both alleged and proven (i.e., conviction
meted out) public police violence, each community's response to the
events reflects its own experience with the police, the government, and
other public organizations. In most incidents, the public's perception was
primarily filtered through the eyes of the media and conditioned by similar historically significant cases.

In the events previously discussed, the police's ability to "prove" the
criminal intent or actions of the victim(s) and the results of judicial decisions, not the existence (or lack) of incontrovertible documentation of
police violence, were essential factors in determining the outcome of the
situation. These factors, on average, determine whether the police accept
wrongdoing by charging or punishing their officers or demonstrate com-
mitment to implement future changes in police policies and practices.
These two criteria are, however, necessary but not sufficient to effect
change. Although two incidents were videotaped, providing what many
people would consider fool-proof evidence that would have made a
courtroom debate about the guilt of the accused officers unequivocal,

each police force could not "reliably" identify all of the officers involved in the misconduct, and most escaped disciplinary and/or criminal charges. Nevertheless, the tapes occasioned some effect (i.e., reprimands and some transfers and apologies), but not the outcomes that such damaging evidence was expected to provoke.

In other words, both criteria cited above (i.e., guilt of the police officer and/or criminal record of the victim) were neither necessary nor sufficient for change in the police departments investigated. Only when the officer's misconduct was perceived by upper management to be unacceptable (i.e., the police riot incidents) was an officer punished.

The findings in those cases where victims had in fact committed criminal actions (i.e., Evans, Perry, Turner, and Davidson) are more ambiguous. Of these, only the two torture cases led to criminal charges being laid against the police officers; only in the South Ozone stun gun torture events did it lead to a criminal conviction of the officers. It is reassuring that in democratic societies safeguards exist that try to ensure that even criminals or those charged with criminal offenses cannot be brutalized with impunity by the extractors of confessions.

Changes in police policies, procedures, and personnel occurred as a result of incidents that were later decided in a criminal trial and other situations that stopped short of a criminal investigation. Another interesting factor—the relation of which to the other above-mentioned criteria at this point is difficult to assess—is that in those cases with irrefutable evidence, the victim(s) were generally young, numerous, middle-class, and white. It was only in some of these events that criminal charges were laid against the officers involved, and some, albeit narrow, policy changes were implemented. This may reflect a police bias for action when the victims of police violence do not fit common expectations (i.e., individuals who are young black males). This finding is not surprising given police officers' class, ethnic, racial, and socioeconomic backgrounds and aspirations. This subtle but pointedly displayed bias is characteristic of police both in Toronto and New York City (see Table 5.5).

One way to interpret the low-level public, governmental, and police arousal, reaction, and outcomes to these events is to see it as a manifestation of three interrelated processes. In particular, it might be a manifestation of alienation, apathy, cynicism, non-participation, political inefficiency, or avoidance (as specified in the model). Alternatively, the low amounts can also be viewed as reflecting an automatic acceptance, obedience, or deference to authority. The low level of arousal, reaction, and outcomes could also be the product of sublimated frustration, which may be vented only after a "sufficient" number of events has occurred. These three complementary interpretations will be discussed in the following section.

Table 5.5
Responses to Three Different Types of Police Violence

Deadly Force	Torture	Police Riots
Officer not criminally charged	Officer(s) criminally charged	Officer(s) not criminally charged
Coroner's inquest	Investigation by Internal Affairs	Police summon videotapes
Police and their lawyers play up criminal record of victim, criminal nature of the event, and/or hospitalization of police officer	Police and their lawyers play up criminal record of victim	Incident never made it to court
Victim(s) lawyers tried to play up the racial nature of the shootings		
Anti-police demonstration complaint	Pro-police demonstration	Complaints launched at civilian bureau
No convictions	Some convictions	Demotions and forced early retirement
No reported changes in policy and procedure	No reported changes in policy and procedure	Proposals and initiatives for better training

INTERPRETATIONS AND IMPLICATIONS FROM BOTH TYPES OF ANALYSES

Sublimated Frustration That Is Periodically Vented through Protest Only After a Sufficient Number of Events Have Taken Place[4]

Why do communities occasionally protest against police violence? A variety of reasons can be postulated (e.g., Jenkins and Perrow, 1977; Piven and Cloward, 1977). To begin with, all actors have limited attention spans. After a period of time, salient issues fade or are replaced in the public, police, and governmental collective consciousness. Sometimes a critical event needs to take place before people are motivated to take some form of action. Alternatively, a populace's frustration level may have been increasing over the years, incited by a triggering event. In these cases, any event—such as the Evans or Perry shooting, or even the jury's verdict in the Simi Valley trial of the four officers accused of beating Rodney King—would motivate a public protest reaction from the community. According to Piven and Cloward (1977), although the poor are generally passive, occasionally they

become defiant. They challenge traditional authorities, and the rules laid down by those authorities. They demand redress for their grievances. . . . In each instance, masses of the poor were somehow able, if only briefly, to overcome the shame bred by a culture which blames them for their plight; somehow they were able to break the bonds of conformity enforced by work, by family, by community, by every strand of institutional life; somehow they were able to overcome the fears induced by police, by militia, by company guards. (p. 7)[5]

Thus there was a time when, because of police physical and psychological violence, the visible (primarily black) community acquiesced to the police. As people from lesser developed countries have become the majority in many urban neighborhoods, observers' perceptions about the passive victim have changed. This coincides with New York City activist lawyer Stanley Cohen's observation that "there is a theory in Crown Heights, Bushwick and the Lower East Side that once a year the beast [repressed minorities] has to raise its head and kick ass."[6]

Obedience/Deference to Authority

Closely connected to apathy is acceptance, obedience, or deference to authority (Milgram, 1974). According to Piven and Cloward (1977):

People usually remain acquiescent, conforming to the accustomed patterns of daily life in their community and believing those patterns to be both inevitable and just. . . . Most of the time people conform to the institutional arrangements which enmesh them, which regulate the rewards and penalties of daily life, and which appear to be the only possible reality. Those for whom the rewards are most meager, who are the most oppressed by inequality, are also acquiescent. Sometimes they are the most acquiescent. (p. 6)

Police have authority, in the typical sense of the term; that is, they have the right to command others and the power to do so (Kelman and Hamilton, 1989: 54). Some of the reasons people are deferent or obedient to authority structures such as the police are that "they have little defense against the penalties that can be imposed for defiance" (Piven and Cloward, 1977: 6). Like apathetic responses, obedience to authority may also be a result of cost-benefit calculations that citizens have made to arrive at the conclusion that they have more to lose than gain from criticizing (i.e., protesting against) police violence.

North American cities attract large numbers of minorities and immigrants. Many have a deep-felt distrust of police, but it varies with the ethnic, class, and racial composition of each neighborhood and com-munity in each city. Many newly arrived immigrants, particularly those from developing nations, either reside in the country illegally or fear that their visitor, immigrant, or work status can be easily revoked. They have language problems, and they are less knowledgeable about their consti-tutional rights, all of which makes them shy away from protest. Like-wise, many minorities who are citizens are also relatively silent. Both Toronto and New York City portray themselves as either a "melting pot" or a "vertical mosaic," but they are in fact racially divided, and so are their perceptions of police brutality. In poor, black, and Latino commu-nities, the police are generally not respected, but in wealthy and white communities, the police are usually revered and perceived to represent the thin line between crime and order.

Cultures vary in their relationship with authorities. Thus, one would expect obedience to authority to be different between Canada and the United States. In particular, Canadians are perceived to be more deferent to authority than their American neighbors (e.g., Friedenberg, 1979; Lip-set, 1985). This may explain, in part, the differences in results between the two cities. In Toronto, for example, Kaplan (1967)

found an attitude of deference toward leadership and authority, an attitude not supportive of intense participation. . . . Long-term residence in a city, especially coupled with ownership of substantial property, is sometimes viewed as endow-ing members of "old families" with a degree of authority to which deference is due in the eyes of working-class people and members of minority ethnic groups. In consequence, they have not tended until recently to be very active politically. (pp. 209–211)

As with apathetic responses, to react, citizens must somehow be aware that the police are abusing their power. The question is, then, how do citizens become aware of police wrongdoing? The primary conduit is once again through the media or their community contacts.

Authority also may be obeyed in literal ways that reflect its rejection. A typical incident, I was told when conducting field research, is when a police officer approaches someone drinking a beer in public and then tells the person to get rid of "it." The citizen promptly responds by pouring the beer on the police officer's shoes. Alternatively, when an officer instructs a citizen to get rid of the bottle or can, the citizen throws it on the street. If it is glass, it may break, thus creating a scenario whereby the officer could be interpreted to have instructed the citizen not only to litter but to create a potential hazard. This is a subtle form of citizen resistance or passive-aggressive behavior that increases beat officers' frustration but has minimal effects on the public's ability to change policing.

Apathy[7]

It is popularly assumed that communities that are affected by police violence will protest or complain against its commission as a way to alter economic, political, or social conditions. Most members of the affected communities, however, have a collective memory of repression, powerlessness, and isolation. Thus they might respond with apathy, "a general term used to characterize the mental state of people in democratic countries who did not bother to vote or to inform themselves about political matters" (Ricci, 1984: 154), and a term used interchangeably with alienation, unattachment, marginalization, and isolation (Rosenberg, 1951; Dean, 1970). For example, Russell's survey of citizens who complained about police abuse disclosed that 14 percent were "apathetic potential complainants" who "could not be bothered to become involved in the detailed procedures of making a complaint" (1978: 52). Thus, the apathetic citizen has no other reason than a lack of desire to make a complaint. Bayley and Mendelsohn (1969) found similar results in their study of Denver. They discovered a number of minority persons who did not want to take the time to complain. In their words, "People simply did not want to be bothered, the complaint was not as important as the time [they would] have to devote to it."

Participating involves a series of cost-benefit calculations made by individuals of affected communities, some of whom rationalize that they stand more to lose (i.e., police harassment, absenteeism from work, and lost wages) than gain in criticizing the police, hence their activities are short lived if not nonexistent. In particular, they cannot afford time off from their jobs to protest social injustices that occur in their lives or in their communities.

Apathy may stem from a degree of conformity, a learned belief in the infallibility of authority, ignorance about how to effect change in democratic systems, inequality, or a feeling that "if it does not affect me personally, why get involved" (e.g., Lamb, 1975). This apathy may also be a function of urban rather than rural life. According to Higgens (1977),

Urbanization results in more people living in more and bigger cities [overcrowding], increases the heterogeneity of the population within cities [decreased sense of community], magnifies the tendency of people to segregate themselves into areas that are socially similar, and produces a broader range of problems. One might expect that each of these factors would increase participation and more things to stimulate them to participate. On the other hand, each of these factors can impede participation. (p. 193)

In fact, "the level of citizen participation in city politics has generally been considered to be low compared to participation in provincial and federal politics." Reasons advanced for this low participation include structural features such as the "process of urbanization," the "timing of municipal elections," "the predilection of many municipal councils to hive off some of their functions onto semi-autonomous ad hoc bodies and committees," "to hold council meetings 'in camera,' " "small city councils" (leading to a high ratio of citizens to elected councilors), and municipalities that are "largely concerned with non-controversial 'house-keeping roles' " (Hanson and Slade, 1977).

While affected communities may not react to police violence, they may respond to other issues that are also politically salient but have more immediate economic impact, such as rent hikes, transit strikes, re-zoning proposals, and so on. Alternatively, apathy may also be disguising a more real, potentially damaging factor; that is, people may not be aware of police abuse of power.

As this study demonstrates, the majority of incidents of police violence receive little media attention. Unless the case is "sensational," articles about police abuse are often relegated to the "metro" or back portion of the newspaper and/or given little space, becoming almost lost among other, well-covered "news events" (e.g., entertainment and sports). On the other hand, those events that receive considerable media attention do raise people's concerns regarding controversial police practices which, in turn, may lead to public unrest.

Many commentators believe that apathy is dysfunctional in a democratic society. Apathetic citizens do not participate in the political system and fail to assist the criminal justice system when it is conducting criminal investigations and prosecutions. In particular, apathetic citizens avoid acting as witnesses or reporting offenses because of fear of reprisal by perpetrators, fear or hatred of the police, or a belief that the criminal justice system can do little about crime. On the other hand, some researchers (e.g., Grodzins, 1956; Converse, 1964; McClosky, 1964) have suggested that apathy can be pro-social. These scholars suggest that forcing the typically apathetic to participate may motivate the political system into introducing irrational policies and practices.

Summary of Implications

These implications explain the pattern of reaction to public police violence in the two cities under observation. This book concludes with a discussion of the ramifications of its findings for some of the wider academic literature.

IMPLICATIONS FOR THE WIDER ACADEMIC LITERATURE

In view of both the quantitative and qualitative results, what are the implications of this study for conventional areas of the social sciences?

The findings have significant meaning for eight overlapping areas of research. In increasing order of importance, they are: organizational theory, public administration, urban politics, state theory, democratic theory, outcomes research, process models, and political participation.

First, police organizations may not necessarily have a tendency toward maintenance or resistance to change when confronted by citizens or their representatives venting sublimated frustration. However, the public, through the combined processes of apathy and obedience to authority, might give organizations the ammunition they need to create a maintenance-like structure. Thus, doubt may be cast on Sherman's (1983) finding that crisis breaks up long-established routines. Granted, organizations are comfortable and familiar with old patterns, but it might be through a natural process of organizational development, not irregularities, that instead leads to change.

Second, many of the responses to citizens' and politicians' demands (e.g., the creation of new or the revitalization of old monitoring organizations, policies, and procedures) may have been more the result of an independent proliferation of bureaucratic functions than of political pressures. Thus even though each police department has its own citizens complaint bureau to which people can appeal, increased external demands placed on the police organization, along with economic pressures, may have forced the Toronto police, for example, to devolve some of their power; it might be more economically or politically expedient for the police to form a separate department, such as the OPCC. One interviewee indicated that he spent a great deal of his time trying to convince the police of the benefits of forming an independent complaints process, on the grounds that if the police were as complaint free as they claimed, this organization would only serve to legitimate this self-held perception.[8]

Third, while some municipal politicians and candidates for public office tried to draw attention to the events of public police violence covered in this study—especially when sublimated frustration led to protest—none of these incidents were sufficient to initiate an urban reform movement (e.g., Lowi, 1967). The management of the police is a contentious urban political issue, and politicians often take a middle position between criticism and support. For example, while Toronto's former mayor Art Eggleton took a moderate approach to the police, John Sewell and Jack Layton traditionally have been very critical. Sewell, in fact, was defeated in a reelection mainly based on his criticism of the police, while Layton lost his bid at the mayoralty, among other reasons, because he was perceived to be the anti-police candidate. Meanwhile, June Rowlands, the former head of the Police Commission, was decidedly pro-police and was eventually elected mayor. In general, only those actors (e.g., reform candidates) who thought they could extract benefits (i.e., votes) protested against police violence.

Fourth, lack of citizen participation (as interpreted here based on the minimal general reaction to police brutality) has implications for democratic theory. In particular, it buttresses the second and third face of power theories of democracy (Bachrach and Baratz, 1962; Lukes, 1974). Perhaps the police have, through the combined processes of public relations and mobilization of bias, prevented the public and other members of the government from voicing their concerns, or have shaped their methods of participation, such that their discontent is deflected or suppressed.

Fifth, some of the most important implications of study are for state theory. Control is manifested in responsiveness to and appeasement of the public. Police forces appear to be motivated to change or do something that approximates citizens' wishes when there is a perception that too much police violence has taken place; when members of certain groups are targeted more than others; when police violence was unjust; when the police force might be sued; and when there is great public outcry. These conditions make the issue of police violence more salient and better defined for the community of concern.

Sixth, despite the periodic changes made to police policies regarding riot situations, there were no detectable differences in broader police policies at the local or national levels (areas where outcomes research has traditionally made a contribution). While challenging groups, in particular, CIRPA and CCLA in Toronto and the NYCLU in New York City, lobbied aggressively for an independent review of police actions, they did not immediately obtain one. Some adjustments have been made in the New York CCRB in terms of board composition; these changes, however, occurred years later and were not necessarily related to earlier incidents of police violence. In addition to the lobbying of earlier years, other factors such as co-optation and burnout led to the implementation of a relatively independent review board in Toronto. Contrary to the opinion of activists, particularly those once connected to CIRPA, who were interviewed for this study, it was primarily the provincial government's work that led to the limited changes and eventually to the establishment of the OPCC.

Changes in riot tactics (both cities) and complaints procedures (Toronto only) were partially in response to community protest. Ultimately money had to be allocated to Toronto's OPCC; there was no corollary in the New York City case. While outcomes research cannot sufficiently or adequately address those unobservable processes that might cause nonaction, non-participation, or apathy on the part of the public, government, or police actors, one can argue that apathy falls somewhere between a conditioning factor and an outcome. It is not a very effective one, but it needs to be addressed. Police violence can prompt the government to launch judicial inquiries, royal commissions, and so on. But the recommendations from these bodies of inquiry are rarely or immediately implemented. The creation of an independent CRB in Toronto is an exception; it required several similar shootings and official inquiries before changes were made to the way in which complaints were investigated and disposed of.[9]

The outcomes of public police violence suggest that police activities are controlled some of the time, under certain conditions, and that increased control depends on a unique constellation of internal and external processes that varies with each case. It can thus be argued that police forces usually act autonomously, buttressing not only arguments of autonomy of the state theorists but also contributing to the creation of a Garrison State (e.g., Lasswell, 1941, 1962; Takagi, 1974).

Seventh, apathy, deference/obedience to authority, and sublimated frustration that manifests itself in occasional protest are not separate actions. They can act in concert to explain the typical responses to police violence. The response to police violence is a complicated phenomenon dependent on context. Therefore, we should reject variance theories and continue to regard response to police violence as a process. Building on Piven and Cloward (1977), there are no events in isolation that have led to mass-membership organizations or protest movements.

Eighth, the results of this study suggest that in the majority of incidents of public police violence, apathy among relevant actors appears to be the norm. Moreover, the two cases of peaceful protest occasioned by the Buddy Evans and Edmund Perry shootings had different outcomes. While the Evans shooting contributed to pressure being exerted on the Ontario provincial government to begin an independent civilian review board, the Perry shooting had no comparable effect in New York City or at the New York State level. Moreover, police use of excessive force in these situations did not provoke widespread massive riots in the way police violence did during the 1960s and later. We did not see the type of public backlash that was experienced in other social movements, including the civil rights and anti-poverty movements. All of the protest groups were relatively powerless in Lipsky's (1970) sense of the term.

This finding corresponds with both Banfield's and Meyerson's (1955) and Lipsky's (1970) research. In their study of the attempt to secure public housing in Chicago, Banfield and Meyerson (1955) assert that pressure from relatively powerless groups did not play a significant role in the decision-making process. Alternatively, "Those groups, primarily Negro, which would have most benefited from a strong public housing program, in fact remained relatively passive" (Lipsky, 1970: 8). Lipsky further suggests that "successful and meaningful outcomes of protest are problematic" (p. 1), particularly with "developing program innovations." In his study of rent strikes in New York City, he notes that while "the rent strike organizations can claim to have placed housing maintenance policies in the public spotlight and given reform a saliency which it would not otherwise have enjoyed, their role in reform of administrative procedures was minimal" (p. 86). He adds that "the lack of status and resources that inhibits protest groups from participating in policy-making conferences . . . also helps prevent explicit bargaining between protest leaders and city officials" (p. 175). Nevertheless, these relatively powerless groups did manage to make the problem salient.

Either community members did not consistently complain and/or protest when residents were affected by police violence, or they did not care (essentially a pluralist position); or, people in positions of authority did not allow these issues to get onto the bargaining table through the "mobilization of bias" (essentially a neo-Marxist position). It can also be argued, as Gaventa (1980) has, that the powerful "exercise[s] power over [affected communities] by influencing, shaping or determining [their] . . . very wants [often in non observable ways]" (p. 12). In other words, a process similar to the one proposed by Lukes (1974) and Gaventa (1980) may explain apathy and obedience/deference to authority, or non-participation in general (e.g., Clark, 1965).

This lack of reaction is similar to the psychological process of learned helplessness. Responses to public police violence, however, differ, because unlike the dog who gets shocked no matter how it behaves (here referring to a classic learned helplessness experiment), we witness periodic outbursts of reaction. Even so, this reaction occurs only when similar incidents of police violence take place temporally close to each other and relevant episodic factors such as number, gender, and age and race of victim(s), race of police officer(s), and perception of illegality surround the incident. Only then do the police or government implement some kind of changes in the criminal justice and legal systems. For the most part, however, there exists a historical memory that fighting against "the system"—if not a fruitless endeavor—pays very small dividends for the effort invested.

This interpretation is also similar to research on voting in the United States, wherein only a little over half of the eligible population votes in presidential elections and fewer still vote in off-year contests (e.g., Piven and Cloward, 1988). Explanations of non-voting are roughly of two kinds: theories that attribute it to political processes and those that locate the causes of absenteeism outside of politics. The latter tradition consists of numerous studies that ascribe the constriction of the active electorate to the social or psychological characteristics of the non-voters themselves.

Applying this reasoning to police violence and reactions to it, we might be witnessing a process whereby concerned communities are socialized into apathy because of previous failures when attempting to change the system. Looking at the qualitative analysis, we get a clearer picture of the type of reactions that transpired and whether there were

Figure 5.1
Implications of Apathy, Deference to Authority/Obedience to Authority, and Sublimated Frustration Which Is Periodically Interrupted by Political Participation

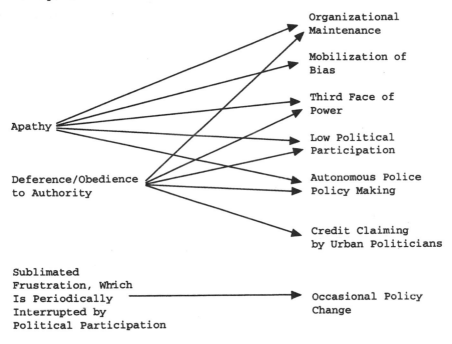

any tangible outcomes in policy or otherwise (see Figure 5.1). However, it may be safe to assume that if there was a reaction, it would have had some, albeit limited, effect on the police or governmental bodies responsible for supervising the police.

AVENUES OF FURTHER STUDY

If apathy, obedience/deference to authority, and sublimated frustration that are periodically vented through protest only after a sufficient number of events have occurred, is the prevailing interpretation of these results, and assuming that in a democracy these are not appropriate citizen responses to police use of excessive force, then those of us interested in ameliorating police violence might consider several options. Among them are redesigning our political system, implementing methods to increase citizen participation when the community experiences acts of police violence, encouraging the questioning of authority, or developing a mechanism that consistently and/or better informs the public of the amount, type, and nature of police violence.[10]

Some theorists, researchers, and activists believe that a community's police should be representative of that particular locale. In other words, the force should mirror the cultural, ethnic, linguistic, racial, sexual, gender, and religious composition of the jurisdiction served. This, they argue, would ensure that the values and beliefs of the citizenry would be taken into account in the police's decision-making process. In North America, it has been noted that public service agencies have traditionally been slow in employing certain groups. Others argue that the inclusion of different cultures will not make much difference in the decisions and behaviors of the public service because of the powerful effects of in-service socialization. It should be noted, however, that this criticism may not outweigh the benefits of having a police force that can empathize with the populace by virtue of being similar to them. Even if the police officer finds himself or herself with divided loyalties to his or her social group and to the subculture of the police, he or she would still be sensitive to the plight of the members of his or her community.

Building on Thomas Jefferson's dictum that "the price of liberty is eternal vigilance," citizens must learn that change in democratic societies can take place only if they initiate, sustain, and monitor it. Although a number of techniques can be introduced to minimize police violence and in many cases protect police officers, such as photographing, tape recording, or videotaping police-citizen encounters, these practices are not widespread. Nonetheless, wherever possible, and despite the possibility of being mislabeled a state agent, those attending demonstrations should be encouraged to use these apparatuses to document potential incidents of violent (or nonviolent) police-citizen interactions, and police should expand the use of camcorders on police cruisers (as is practiced in some jurisdictions) as well as in the reception areas, holding cells, and carports of police stations where prisoners are escorted back and forth.[11]

Given the paucity of official and unofficial data, a more active press would also help. Making it mandatory for reporters to spend a minimum amount of time on the police beat and encouraging a critical and not primarily co-optative relationship with law enforcement authorities may change the boosterish style of some police reporters. Finally, though difficult to empirically document, the implementation of an independent CRB in some respects could reduce police violence.

Although it is difficult to determine whether police violence will increase in the future (Ross, 1994b), unless we break the pattern of apathy, obedience/deference to authority, and sublimated frustration, which is periodically vented through protest only after a sufficient number of events have taken place, we cannot realistically lessen and control police violence. If the public, government, and law enforcement officials remain complacent, it may well be business as usual for police departments, the government, and citizens alike.

NOTES

1. First, the case summaries for coding could be improved by expanding the scope of sources, including materials from interviews. This depends in part on greater cooperation from sources, particularly police departments and victims. Field work activities such as participant observation, content analyses of the print media (e.g., Beare, 1987), and other forms of news media (e.g., radio and television) could also be explored. Finally, more and better archival sources could be tapped. On the other hand, if the researcher was to expand the scope of the newspaper indexes, he or she would find that it might just increase the amount of missing information. While material is missing on the current pool of cases, certainly new cases will be found that will have more missing information.

Second, the number of years examined could be extended at least to the beginning of 1960, which is compatible with other data sets on violence, particularly in Canada (Ross, 1988, 1992b, 1994a).

Third, the number of cities could be increased. London, England, Sydney, Australia, and Wellington, New Zealand, should be investigated to give the findings wider applicability.

Fourth, the top 10 most popular major newspaper indexes in the world could be identified and, based on the citations, one could determine the acts of police violence that received the top 100 number of citations. Then an analysis could be performed among those at the top and those at the bottom to see if there were any differences. This would alleviate the problems with the nation, state, and city dimensions as areas of comparison. Or the researcher could look at the cases that received the most amount of media reaction over the past 30 years, as measured by the *New York Times Index* to determine which types of cases get what type of response.

Fifth, indexes for each variable must be sharpened. This would be aided by using Guttman scaling techniques (e.g., Nie et al., 1970: ch. 2). A preliminary course of action might be to pre-test the currently constructed indexes on participants in the control system. In other words, one would administer a survey to members of the public, government, and police, asking them to rank order the values in every variable. This would make the scales more generalizable and would indicate future research directions.

2. One might be tempted to exclude variables where there is no consensus in the literature about their level of measurement (e.g., the type of police violence could not be categorized into low, medium, and high for there is little data on what constitutes low, medium, and high violence).

3. While Spearman Rank Correlations should be run on ranked data, SPSS/PC+ does not have this statistic, and the differences between it and the Pearson Correlation are trivial (Glass and Hopkins, 1984: 97).

4. This may be similar to the biological (evolutionary) concept of punctuated equilibrium (e.g., Stephen J. Gould, Niles Elderidge, and Stephen M. Stanley). Although this concept is intriguing, in general, biologists do not seem to be taking it too seriously these days.

5. Piven and Cloward (1977) look at the structuring of protest in general and in four specific cases: the unemployed workers movement, the industrial workers

movement, the civil rights movement, and the welfare rights movement. In general, they criticize the development of organizations to help social movements. According to the authors,

During those brief periods in which people are roused to indignation, when they are prepared to defy the authorities to whom they ordinarily defer, during those brief moments when lower-class groups exert some force against those who call themselves leaders do not usually escalate the momentum of the people's protest. (pp. xxi–xxii)

Additionally, "[O]rganizers not only failed to seize the opportunity presented by the rise of unrest, they typically acted in ways that blunted or curbed the disruptive force which lower-class people were sometimes able to mobilize." The authors stress the institutional boundaries on shaping protest behavior: "People experience deprivation and oppression within a concrete setting . . ."; "institutional patterns shape . . . the collectivity out of which protest can arise"; "determine the strategic opportunities for defiance" (pp. 20–21). The demise of the protest is accounted for by a number of reasons, including the granting of concessions and isolation from potential supporters.

6. Based on a personal interview with Stanley Cohen, August 29, 1991.

7. Apathy is closely connected to alienation, but the work on alienation and political activity, or lack of it, is contradictory (e.g., Kraus and Davis, 1980: 181–183).

8. Based on a personal interview with Roy McMurtry, December 30, 1991.

9. Among the controls that many jurisdictions and countries have instituted are Ombudsmen (e.g., Denmark, New Zealand, Great Britain, and Canada) or public complaints commissioners who are independent from the police but have investigatory powers. Many academics, activists, and lawyers disliked such mechanisms. They felt that ministerial or supervisor responsibility should be uppermost.

10. Lane (1959), for example, advocated more political participation, education, and personal income so that citizens would act to benefit the masses.

11. Police are also using this technique for their own benefit; they are experimenting with tape-recording interrogations with arrestees to prevent malicious prosecution cases. See, for example, Grant (1980) and Baldwin (1992) for an explanation of this process.

Appendix A

Research Design and Methodology

CASE SELECTION

Countries to Focus On

Police violence takes place in all countries of the world. However, because the data on this controversial practice and because measures of response are nonexistent, unreliable, too costly to collect, or plagued with jurisdictional and mandate vagaries among different police forces, an appropriate sample was selected.

Although it might be informative to look at the effects of police violence in a variety of disparate systems, the methodological problems mentioned above make this option difficult. These challenges are minimized by using a most similar systems design. Although communist, authoritarian, and/or lesser developed states have been routinely identified as having a greater incidence of police violence than first-world countries, data from non-Western countries is generally unreliable (Bayley, 1971, 1979, 1985). Adding to this problem is the fact that police forces in these countries differ substantially in mandates and compositions within and among them. Consequently, this investigation was narrowed down to first-world, advanced, industrialized democracies.

Governments in these types of countries usually have a high degree of legitimacy, and their coercive organizations usually work within the framework of law. When intolerable levels of police violence come to public attention, there is often public police and governmental arousal. Moreover, the nature of these political systems, unlike the authoritarian regimes, facilitates the expression of public discontent through a variety of ways, especially the media. Consequently, information on the incidence of public police violence and reactions to it in first-world countries are easier to obtain and more reliable. Yet there are many states that are subsumed by the first-world, advanced, industrialized democracies label.

Three types of advanced, industrialized democratic states can be identified: Western, non-Western, and Anglo-American. Of the three, Anglo-American democracies were selected to maximize a most similar systems design. Due to the greater number of similarities among this set of countries, incidents of public police violence in two Anglo-American democracies, namely the United States and Canada, was identified. Great Britain, Australia, and New Zealand were excluded because of the increased costs in acquiring data and the perceived minimal additional benefits to the main purpose of this study.

In general, both countries have similar polities and political institutions. In particular, American and Canadian police forces are relatively similar in structure. On the other hand, each of these countries has a multiplicity of police forces at the municipal, regional, provincial, and/or state levels. These differences create ecological difficulties such as variations in force structure, size, and composition of police. The communities policed vary not only between countries but also among jurisdictions within a state. Moreover, this complexity creates data-gathering difficulties. The most similar system design best lends itself to investigating urban locales, particularly large ones with similar populations. The assumption would then be that differences in the results should be explainable in part by historical, legal, political, and social differences among cities.

Cities to Focus On

Although the case study approach has advantages and disadvantages (e.g., Eckstein, 1975; Lijphart, 1971, 1975), knowing which cases to select is difficult. Ideally, researchers could compare several similar police departments and their communities. One strategy might be to choose cities that have, over a significant period of time, the highest rates of police use of deadly force. However, there is no reason to believe that the incidence of deadly force is highly correlated with police violence in general.

Two police forces and the communities that they serve, however, make natural comparisons; those of New York City and Toronto. Each city is a national and an international center of business, culture, and government, and each is a "melting pot" of many races and ethnic and religious groups. These metropolises have the largest populations and police forces in their province or state, region and country. Their law enforcement agencies are also what Fogelson (1977) refers to as big-city police forces. Most important, each city is perceived to have had an increase in police violence against its citizens.

The Toronto Police Force (TPF), incorporated in 1834, was amalgamated in 1957 into the Metropolitan Toronto Police Force (MTPF) with the "cities" of Toronto, York, Etobicoke, North York, Scarborough, and the borough of East York, collectively referred to as the Municipality of Metropolitan Toronto. In 1989, it had an authorized strength of 5,489 police and 1,960 civilian personnel to "serve and protect" 2,160,000 citizens, which means roughly one police officer for almost every 400 citizens. Policing a city of this size, with a diverse population, has resulted in many problems of police violence (see Chapter 3).

Although it was not the first police force developed in America, the New York Police Department (NYPD) is one of the oldest. Created in 1845, it is responsible for patrolling the boroughs of Manhattan, Staten Island, Queens, the Bronx, and Brooklyn. Its presence is magnified by its association with the transit and public housing police, comprising 4,214 and 2,037 members, respectively. In 1989, it had an authorized strength of 26,043 police and 9,755 civilian personnel to provide service to approximately 8 million citizens. This means that there is approximately one police officer per 307 citizens, making it one of the most heavily policed cities in North America. Like its Canadian counterpart, the NYPD has been brought into the public spotlight through a variety of incidents of police violence that made headlines from 1977 to 1990 (see Chapter 4).

Data on Public Police Violence

The model of responses to public police violence identifies a number of individuals, organizations, and processes. Many of the activities conducted in closed organizational settings such as police departments can be revealed only by using ethnographic methodology (see, e.g., Manning, 1977, 1983, 1985). These methods have several advantages and disadvantages.

Regardless, although public police violence can be conceptualized through reports of violent acts committed or alleged to have been conducted by police, as documented in officers' notes, citizen/witness complaints, and media attention, not only are officers' notes and citizen witnesses' complaints inaccessible to most researchers, their connection to the process of publicity that is requisite for an action to serve the agenda-setting function is unknown.

In the main, data on police violence can be obtained from case studies, governmental reports, survey/public opinion/victimization research, police files, court records, observational studies, police misconduct/complaints statistics, deaths in custody tabulations, and police use of deadly force data. Unfortunately, these sources contain little or no data on public police violence that is either publicly available, detailed, systematic, adequate, objective, reliable, comprehensive (in terms of time and location), sufficient, comparable, and/or nonreactive enough to test hypotheses on the process of public police violence.

Methods that overcome the previously mentioned shortcomings are preferable. For these reasons, on-site observational methods were not undertaken in this study. The unobtrusive methodologies of events data research and thick descriptive analysis are used instead. Both methods shed light on those aspects of policing that are inaccessible to ethnographic researchers.

EVENTS DATA METHODOLOGY

Introduction

In events data research, each act of public police violence can be conceptualized as an episode consisting of a series of stages, actions, or effects, which are similar to those measured in the conflict processes literature (see, e.g., McAdam, 1982). Although the advantages and disadvantages of events data research can be debated, it was used as a counterbalance to the qualitatively based thick descriptive portion of this study.

Creating the Events Database

To maximize the reliability and validity in collecting data on the process of public police violence and reaction to it, an events data set was created. This entailed creating a chronology of public police violence that included the series of reactions to each episode in each city. Each event was coded on significant variables (see Appendix B), and the statistical analysis of many hypothesized relationships between these variables was conducted.

Preferable and Actual Sources of Information

The chronology on public police violence based on newspaper article citations was compiled, but it is not without its limitations. First, there are a plethora of newspapers from which to choose. Second, some are perceived to be more biased than others (especially in favor of police). Third, newspapers vary in the amount of coverage they give to police issues. Fourth, and most important, some newspapers are not easily accessible. Three newspapers and their respective indexes that minimize these difficulties were chosen for this purpose. They include: the *New York Times Index* (for articles written on the NYPD) and the *Canadian*

News Index (CNI) (for articles written in the *Globe & Mail* and *Toronto Star* on the MTPF).

To test the model, instances of police violence were documented with special attention to the variables that are mainly associated with public, governmental and police arousal, reaction, and outcomes. This meant looking at the process that takes place after incidents of public police violence occur. All citations listed in the newspaper indexes under the heading "Police" or related subjects (e.g., "Charges Against," "Police Benevolent Association," etc.) that seemed to indicate acts and responses to police violence taking place in these two cities were recorded. Invariably, several incidents garnered a considerable amount of publicity and directed the reader to look elsewhere in the index to a separate section (e.g., under the general heading of "demonstrations and riots, police handling" or under the names of particular recipients of police violence). These other subheadings provided additional sources of relevant citations. Classifications listed after the heading "Police," which included police-related institutions (e.g., Police Federation), also were surveyed, and appropriate citations were transcribed. Since most entries provided scant information on the episode, each article from microfilmed issues of the three papers was photocopied. All of the pertinent information regarding the allegation was assembled into a detailed chronology. This process required reading approximately 1,500 separate newspaper articles.

Time Frame

The starting point, 1977, was chosen for two major reasons. First, the *CNI* did not begin publication until 1977. Second, 1977 serendipitously and roughly corresponds with the beginning of what some observers consider the post-material (silent revolution) era, characterized by distinctive political, economic, and social problems (Ingelhart, 1977). The period from 1977 to 1990 provides a long enough time frame to make meaningful comparisons and deal with some difficulties of previous research. The time frame under investigation includes different police and city administrations and political parties in power, allowing for some internal variation. In 1990, Ontario's *Police Services Act* was passed, and Lee Brown began as the new Police Chief of New York City. Thus December 1990 serves as a convenient cutoff point. In sum, a 14-year time frame, from January 1, 1977, to December 31, 1990, inclusive, was examined.

Inclusion/Exclusion Criteria

All news items that could be interpreted as police violence or responses to this type of police behavior were recorded. Every attempt was made to order the stages of each event in a chronological fashion. Since several incidents of police violence stretch over a number of years, it was necessary to track each individual event, from allegation to charge/dismissal/trial/verdict, outcome, and policy change (if any). For instance, an allegation of police abuse often takes a number of years before it comes to trial if it results in this outcome.

All citations of articles regarding police violence were recorded, excluding letters to the editor, if they were listed. Even though letters to the editor are important in the development of an issue and are listed in the *New York Times Index*, these items are excluded from the *CNI*. Hence, they were omitted to avoid problems of comparable data. Moreover, an event taking place before 1977 but reported in or after 1977 was also disregarded.

Additionally, actions by police officers while they were off duty were omitted despite their suspension from the force, pending criminal charge, or nonpolice reactions. Moreover, actions by police officers that were recorded in the media as accidents (e.g., unintentional firing of guns, running over pedestrians with their cars, shooting of partner/s, etc.) are also excluded.

Last, violent actions by civilian employees of the police departments were not included. Although generating a great deal of controversy, they are not the actions of sworn-in police officers engaged in the performance of their legal duties. If the date of the incident was not specified, it was assumed to have taken place on the day preceding the publication of the article. And when the race of a victim was not given, it was inferred from the surname or other surrounding information where possible. When this was not determined it was coded as missing.

Coding Procedures

The choice of variables, hypotheses, and statistical tests was a function of the previously outlined model, my ability to operationalize as many variables from that model and find appropriate data for testing, and the quality of the data that was assembled. Although carefully specified hypotheses are necessary in any research endeavor, data/indicators for each of the variables originally specified may be difficult or impossible to obtain.

To achieve a comprehensive picture of the model, ideally one should examine the scope, nature, and intensity of each act of public police violence and the response/s to its occurrence. This is not an easy endeavor, because public police violence and its outcomes are a lengthy, complex, and often covert process. Variables previously outlined were coded from the chronology on the most severe action that took place (see Appendix B). For example, a beating that also involved a shooting was coded only as a shooting. Perceptions of the illegality of the episode were established through respondents' statements (i.e., people interviewed in articles) or judicial actions. In sum, a total of 65 events of public police violence in New York City and 51 events in Toronto was identified.

Statistical Tests: Exploratory Analysis

Ultimately, the statistical tests performed depended upon the quality of the data. Using the number of articles generated as the only available measure of arousal, a three-way categorization of cases was performed by dividing the population of total articles on each event generated into minimal arousal (one article only), medium arousal (two to four articles), and high arousal (five or more articles). Then cross-tabs and chi-square tests of significance were performed for all incident variables previously specified in the model. Chi-square analyses of relationships between arousal and response variables were limited to cases with medium or high arousal (greater then two articles published). Even though all attempts were made to use similar sources of data, the New York City and Toronto samples were kept distinct in the comparisons, since there is no theoretical or empirical reason to believe that the relationship should be the same in both cities.

THICK DESCRIPTIVE METHODOLOGY

Introduction

Thick descriptive methods include that body of techniques that encompasses archival research, documentation analysis, and interviews with informants and secondary source subjects (Geertz, 1973). Although there are advantages and disadvantages with this methodology, it was seen as a necessary counterbalance to the quantitative events data portion of the study (Ragin, 1987).

Conducting the Thick Descriptive Analysis

The thick descriptive part of this study was enhanced by the use of a pilot case study (i.e., the Denver Police Department). This helped sensitize me to problems that might be encountered in the field and to additional questions that should be asked. Cooperation from informants and secondary sources was enhanced in this setting, because the individuals were advised that the research would not show up in the final study.

Three similar cases of public police violence from each city, obtained from the data set (a total of six) that generated the greatest amount of media attention (i.e., the highest number of newspaper citations) and categorized into three different types of police violence (i.e., police riot, deadly force, and torture) were selected for intensive "thick descriptive" analysis; these episodes were reconstructed by the author.

Documentation and Archival Research

Several kinds of sources were examined to flesh out more details and to give a better contextual analysis. These sources can be divided into written and human types. Written sources can be further categorized between archival and public domain materials. The former included city records, selected vertical files of news clippings at various libraries (e.g., the Centre for Criminology at the University of Toronto), and correspondence between the police department and city politicians, sometimes found in city and police archives. The latter public domain materials included reports of public inquiries, royal commissions, police department annual reports, government publications, local histories, police histories, newspapers, Attorney/Solicitor General reports, newsletters and pamphlets of concerned groups (e.g., police monitoring groups such as the CIRPA), and the Police Union/Association magazine for each force.

Informants and Secondary Source Subjects

It was necessary to interview people involved in and responding to many of the acts of police violence documented through the chronology and secondary source material. Attempts were made to conduct unstructured face-to-face, semi-structured interviews with as many people as possible who could provide information on the policy and practices of the police and the incidents selected for intensive case study in each city.

Some of the formal controllers who were sought for interviews were the Chiefs of Police, Solicitor/Attorney Generals, chairs of important Commissions on the Police, and members of the Police Complaints Board. Interviews were also conducted with representatives or directors of several nongovernmental organizations that exerted a measure of informal control over the police: civil liberties organizations, police associations/unions, and the media. Finally, an attempt was made to speak to members and leaders of community groups and political parties regarding their opinions and experience dealing with the police; people who had been involved in these struggles (victims, police officers, activists, lawyers, etc.); and police reporters who were responsible for writing the majority of the articles on the police during the time period under investigation.

The names of people to be interviewed were initially culled from the chronology of public police violence assembled from the previously mentioned newspapers, literature read on this topic, and those sources suggested by the people contacted. An attempt was made to contact every person mentioned in the chronology and those suggested by others as someone to whom I should speak.[1] An attempt also was made to talk to the present and past heads of comparable organizations in each city. A series of trips was made to each city, which refocused the collection of written materials and questions to be asked and provided the opportunity to interview more sources. The majority of interviews was arranged through correspondence and/or telephone calls. Notes were taken or photocopies were made of archival items, depending upon the volume of the material. Interviews took one-half hour to two hours. Tape recordings were not made, but notes were taken when the situation permitted; otherwise, notes were made after each interview.

Although as many people as possible were contacted, those heading or working for public and private organizations during the events that generated the most newspaper citations were given priority. Informants were granted anonymity unless they requested or agreed to attribution. Undoubtedly, they constituted a biased sample, since they were the only people who wished to grant me some time and may have had a variety of motives for talking with me. The visits did not allow me the time to cultivate forthcoming higher-level sources inside of the respective police departments. Follow-up interviews and additional interviews were often conducted over the telephone. (see note 1).

Ultimately, all of the techniques used by investigative journalists were used. This included the cultivation of as many sources as possible, the acquisition of internal memos, both confidential and nonroutine, the protection of sources, starting with the least controversial question first, and in some cases the misrepresentation of the research question. The guiding principle was to be creative in source acquisition, development, and questions asked.

NOTE

1. A total of 129 individuals were contacted. Fifty-three agreed to be interviewed, and the balance provided polite excuses for why they could not participate.

Appendix B

Coding Sheet Used to Record and Categorize the Variables in the Process Model

PUBLIC POLICE VIOLENCE CODING SHEET EPISODE CHARACTERISTICS

1. ____ City where event took place (ignore out-of-jurisdiction violence)
   1. NYC
   2. Toronto

2. ____ Day event took place (If it involves a series of events, then date of first event)

3. ____ Month event took place

4. ____ Year event took place

5. ____ Number of articles that the incident generated (limited to *NYT* and *G&M/TS*)

6. ____ Days elapsed between printing of first and last article

7. ____ Number of victims in incident

8. ____ Public figure victim(s) (e.g., respected member of community, infamous person)
   1. Yes
   2. No
   999. Missing

9. ____ Gender of victim(s)
   1. Female
   2. Male
   3. Mixed (i.e., victims were both)
   999. Missing

10. ____ Gender of police officer(s)
          1.   Female
          2.   Male
          3.   Mixed
          999. Missing

11. ____ Race of victim(s)
          1.   White
          2.   Minority (visible)
          3.   Mixed
          999. Missing

12. ____ Race of police officer(s)
          1.   White
          2.   Minority (visible)
          3.   Mixed
          999. Missing

13. ____ Weight of victim(s) (if more than one victim, code
          total)
          999. Missing

14. ____ Weight of police officer(s) (if more than one
          officer, code total)
          999. Missing

15. ____ Severity (degree of harm to victim(s) coded on the
          most severe action)
          1.   Beating (includes assault)
          2.   Brutality (unspecified/miscellaneous)
          3.   Torture
          4.   Deadly force (may or may not result in death)
          5.   Killing (unspecified/miscellaneous)
          999. Missing

16. ____ Activity level of victim(s)
          1.   If victim(s) was passive (includes handcuffed)
               and running away
          2.   If victim(s) was active (put up resistance)
          3.   If victim carried a weapon (includes fake)
          999. Missing

17. ____ Demeanor of subject
          1.   Intoxicated
          2.   High on drugs
          3.   Mentally ill
          4.   Physically impaired
          999. Missing

18. ____ Age of officer(s) (if more than one officer, code
          the total)

19. ___   Age of victim(s) (if more than one victim, code the
            total)
            999. Missing

20. ___   Number of victims (reported as being physically
            affected by the violence)
            999. Missing

21. ___   Number of police engaging in violence
            999. Missing

22. ___   Moral/controversial setting (Did the action take
            place within an environment that could be
            considered moral [e.g., abortion clinic protest]?)
            1.   Yes
            2.   No
            3.   Undeterminable
            999. Missing

23. ___   Perception of illegality
            1.   Criminal charge against officer(s) was
                 discussed
            2.   Criminal charge was not discussed
            3.   Undetermined
            999. Missing

24. ___   Scope (how many actors get involved beyond victim[s]
            and police officer[s] and department). Reflects number
            of people interviewed in articles who are
            representatives of organizations.

REACTION/S OF ACTORS

25. ___   National Police Research and Interest Organization(s)
            999. Missing

26. ___   Private businesses and their associations
            1.   Insurance company extends policy to Police
                 Department
            2.   Insurance company threatens to cancel policy
                 on the Police Department
            3.   Merchants demand reinstatement of police
                 officer(s)
            999. Missing

27. ___   Police union/association(s)
            1.   Complains to Police Department or press
            2.   Files grievance
            3.   Sues court
            4.   Holds press conference
            5.   Appeals the decision to the Supreme Court

      6.   Threatens injunction to block the measure
      7.   Demonstration in support of officer(s) on trial
    999. Missing

28. ___ Elected official(s)
      1.   District Attorney investigates
      2.   District Attorney probes event
      3.   Mayor comments/complains against police
      4.   Mayor/state official requests investigation
      5.   District Attorney accuses police
      6.   Assemblyperson questions police discipline
      7.   City council urges hiring/adding new recruits
      8.   Mayor visits family of victims
      9.   Representative criticizes police work in matter
    10.   NDP leader calls for new investigation
    11.   NDP leader promises to push public inquiry
    12.   Liberal attempts to calm protest by positive comments about improvement in black/police relations
    13.   Liberal M.P. says Solicitor General is violating the law
    14.   Mayor's office says investigation will be conducted
    999. Missing

29. ___ Citizen group/s and/or organization/s
      1.   Citizen/s group forms
      2.   Citizen/s group/s complains
      3.   Public demonstration
      4.   Citizen/s (nonvictim/s) complain (unspecified recipient)
      5.   Citizen/s group/s call for public inquiry
      6.   Citizen/s group holds news conference
      7.   Pro-police group holds rally
      8.   Pro-police group holds counter demonstration
      9.   Residents demand reinstatement of police officer/s
    10.   Former president of Police Association criticized complaint system
    11.   Citizen/s group holds news conference and calls for public inquiry
    999. Missing

30. ___ Media (Newspaper)
      1.   Editorial favoring court decision
      2.   Editorial telling police to weed out "bad apples"
      3.   Journalist supports police actions
      4.   Editorial proposes civilians on Police Board

5.   Journalist criticizes police unwillingness to confirm complaints on fellow officers
6.   Neutrally describes event
7.   Mentions that elements of incident were broadcast on television
8.   Columnist suggests that citizen interest groups must be heard
9.   Columnist writes critique of event
10. Columnist suggests that officers have fabricated evidence
11. Columnist says procedures are not being respected
999. Missing

31. ___   Victim/s or relative/s
1.   Sues police/launches civil action
2.   Launches complaint with police complaints division
3.   Sends letter to ombudsman
4.   Sends letter to Police Commission
5.   Sends letter to Solicitor General/Attorney General
6.   Tells story to the newspaper
7.   Announces this to a police inquiry
8.   Launches complaint to the Provincial/State Police Commission
9.   Launches complaint with the Police Department's Police Commission
10. Lays charge against the police officer(s)
11. Contacts elected representative
12. Hires lawyer
13. Launches miscellaneous complaint
999. Missing

32. ___   Government Agencies
1.   Court/Justice/Crown considers law to apply
2.   Court/Justice/Crown lays charge
3.   Court/Justice/Crown/Jury convicts officer(s)
4.   Court/Justice/Crown/Jury convicts officer(s) of all charges
5.   Court/Justice/Crown/Jury convicts officer(s) of some charges
6.   Court/Justice/Crown/Jury acquits officer(s)
7.   Court/Justice/Crown upholds acquittal
8.   Court/Justice/Crown sentences officer(s)
9.   U.S. Attorney office probes allegation(s)
10. Court/Justice/Crown awards victim(s) financial compensation
11. Prisons sentence(s) suspended

12. Appeals Court strikes down lower court ruling on sentence to officer(s)
13. Charges are dropped
14. Grand jury investigates
15. Jury acquits officer(s)
16. Jury finds accused guilty/sentence given
17. Jurors comment that the case was not well presented
18. Coroner gives decision
19. Accused is exonerated
20. Sentences officer and awards victim financial compensation
21. Court/Justice/Crown lays charge and Grand Jury investigates
22. Complaint board official criticizes slow procedure
999. Missing

33. ____ Accused officer/s
1. Appeals departmental decisions
2. Performs community work in advance of sentence
3. Sues court
4. Appeals court decision
5. Suppresses facts or provides false information surrounding case/refused to allow questioning
6. Hires lawyer/s to defend self
7. Pleads not guilty
8. Says victim threatened him/or family by victim's menacing behavior
9. Pleads guilty
10. Sues plaintiff (victim(s))
11. Says victim resisted arrest and refused to show identification
12. Misses inquest
999. Missing

OUTCOMES

34. ____ Police Department public relations and resistance
1. Lifts suspension on officer(s)
2. Suspends investigation
3. Dismisses departmental charge
4. Rejects complaint
5. Publishes figures on its ability to combat crime
6. Holds press conference
7. Threatens job action

8.   Commissioner says officers need more training
9.   Offers a settlement
10. Promises public apology and financial
     retribution
11. Police official blames someone else
12. Police official says victim resisted, was
     aggressive, or was dangerous
13. Chief says department is capable of good
     investigation work into incident
14. Chief says that case is not strong/clear enough
15. Police official says trial was not necessary
16. Chief is ashamed of developments and
     officers' reactions
17. Chief says that victim will file lawsuit
18. Department claims normal procedures were
     respected
999. Missing

35. ___   Internal control initiatives against individual
          officer(s)
1.   Reprimands officer(s)
2.   Agrees to retrain officer(s)
3.   Charges officer(s) with departmental charges
4.   Launches internal investigation
5.   Charges officer(s) with criminal offense
6.   Demotes officer(s)
7.   Reassigns officer(s)
8.   Suspends officer(s) from department
9.   Orders officer(s) to pay damages
10. Dismisses/fires officer(s)
11. Commander is transferred
12. Suspended officer(s) without pay
13. Officer(s) placed on paid leave
14. Orders officer(s) to work without pay
15. Orders officer(s) to resign or be fired
16. Internal affairs investigates
999. Missing

36. ___   Internal control initiatives against entire police
          force
1.   Implements reforms
2.   Reorganizes
3.   Issues policy statement on the use of
     controversial practices
4.   Requests judicial inquest
5.   Orders revision of rules
6.   Implements new regulations
7.   Increases staff of civilian complaints
     division

8.   Releases public report on events
9.   Proposes revision of rules
10. Makes recommendation to committee to review guidelines
999. Missing

37. ___ External official control initiatives against police force (outside the Police Department)
1.   Police Commission launches inquiry
2.   One of a series of complaints that leads to inquiry
3.   Establishes Royal Commission/Senate inquiry
4.   FBI/Solicitor General investigates charges of brutality
5.   City suspends entire Police Department
6.   Government initiates inquest
7.   Government asks third party to intervene
8.   Attorney General advises person to relay charge
9.   Ombudsman orders a new investigation
10. District Attorney investigates
11. District Attorney claims officers are impeding probe
12. Congressional probe
13. Grand jury investigates complaints
14. Coroner releases report with recommendations
15. Commissioner turns down suspension
999. Missing

Appendix C

People Interviewed for the Toronto Portion of the Study

Harold Adamson, former Police Chief

anonymous, friend (#1) of Buddy Evans

anonymous, friend (#2) of Buddy Evans

Avinder Bindra, businessman, involved with Sikh community

Mike Boyd, director, C.O. Bick School, MTPF

Arnold Brunner, lawyer, compiled report on gay/police relations

John Clement, lawyer, compiled report on the police

Mal Connelly, head, Ontario Police Association, formerly head of MTPA

Paul Copeland, civil liberties/criminal lawyer

Mark Dailey, news director, CITY TV

Ari Dassanayake, policy analyst, Ontario Solicitor General

Joan DePeza, director, Metro Committee on Race Relations

Susan Eng, commissioner, Metro Police Commission

Jack Gemmell, lawyer, former member of CIRPA

Philip Givens, retired, former mayor of Toronto and head of Police Commission

Paul Godfrey, publisher, *Toronto Sun*, former Metro controller

Larry Hall, consultant, Hickling-Johnson

Roger Hollender, City Council member

Zuhair Kashmeri, current business reporter, former police reporter, *Globe & Mail*

Bob Kellerman, lawyer

Jack Layton, alderman

Harold Levy, editorial writer, *Toronto Star*

Claire Lewis, commissioner, Civilian Complaints Commissioner

Art Lymer, head, MTPA

Brian McAndrew, editor, *Toronto Star*

Roy McMurtry, lawyer, former Solicitor General of Ontario

Alan Moscoe, City Council member

Jane Pepino, lawyer, former member of Police Commission

Walter Pitman, director of Task Force

Kile Ray, director, 519 Church Street

Charles C. Roach, lawyer

Mike Sale, public affairs officer, MTPF

John Sewell, former mayor

Allan Sparrow, consultant, former alderman

Mark Wainberg, lawyer, former director of CIRPA

Paul Walter, former head of Metro Toronto Police Union

David White, former alderman

Note: Positions of individuals interviewed reflect those held at the time of the study.

Appendix D

People Interviewed for the
New York City Portion of the Study

David Anderson, editor, *New York Times*
Virginia Byrne, reporter, Associated Press
Stanley Cohen, lawyer
Paul DeRienzo, broadcaster, WBAI
Michael Farrin, freelance editor, member of Block A Tenants Association
Mitch Gelman, reporter, *New York Newsday*
Ronald Kuby, lawyer
John Marzulli, reporter, *Daily News*
Peter McGlaughlin, reporter, *Daily News*
James McKinley, reporter, *New York Times*
Anne Murray, reporter, *New York Post*
Clayton Patterson, hatmaker, artist, and videographer
David Pitt, reporter, *New York Times*
Todd Purdum, reporter, *New York Times*
Eric Williams, broadcaster, WBAI

Note: Positions of individuals interviewed reflect those held at the time of the study.

Appendix E

t-Tests for the Samples of City Data

To compare the two samples, a series of independent t-tests on the New York City and Toronto samples was performed. The first scores for "the day the event took place" for the New York group were somewhat more variable than those for the Toronto group. Moreover, for the New York cases, the number of missing values was greater than that for Toronto. This difference in terms of information available may reflect the variability in news reporting between these two cities. A t-test for the paired means was performed to determine if there was a significant difference between New York and Toronto. The null hypothesis of no difference between New York and Toronto was accepted at $p < 0.05$. In other words, the most frequent day when an event took place was the same for New York and Toronto, approximately the 15th of each month.

The t-tests for month of event, number of articles, number of victims involved in the incident, number of police officers engaging in violence, and number of people involved produced no statistically significant differences between them. On the other hand, for both cities, the most popular month for police violence was June; the incidents generated an approximately equal number of articles; the average number of victims was the same; the number of police officers involved was roughly the same; and the number of victims involved in the incident after it took place was small.

However, t-tests performed on both cities for the year the event took place, the age of the victim, the number of victims, and the time elapsed between the first and the last article produced statistically significant differences between the cities. For example, the highest number of events took place in 1983 and 1985 for Toronto and New York City respectively.

In terms of the age of the victim, New York City victims were about 10 years younger than those in Toronto (mean = 30 years old). Significantly, fewer victims were reportedly physically hurt by police violence in Toronto than in New York City, and in New York City the follow-up article was quicker (averaging 14.3 days) than it was for Toronto (averaging 274 days). Despite these findings, the comparisons between these two populations should be treated as heuristic, as data from each of these cases were not exactly the same.

T-TESTS FOR THE SAMPLES OF CITY DATA

Test 1
t-test for DAYEVENT (Day Event Took Place)

	Number of Cases	Mean	Standard Deviation	Standard Error
New York	42	15.33	9.75	1.51
Toronto	44	15.43	7.61	1.15

		Pooled Variance Estimate			Separate Variance Estimate		
F Value	2-Tail Prob.	t Value	Degrees of Freedom	2-Tail Prob.	t Value	Degrees of Freedom	2-Tail Prob.
1.64	.11	-.05	84	.96	-.05	77.54	.96

Test 2
t-test for MONTHEVE (Month Event Took Place)

	Number of Cases	Mean	Standard Deviation	Standard Error
New York	56	6.07	3.58	.48
Toronto	50	6.52	3.49	.49

		Pooled Variance Estimate			Separate Variance Estimate		
F Value	2-Tail Prob.	t Value	Degrees of Freedom	2-Tail Prob.	t Value	Degrees of Freedom	2-Tail Prob.
1.05	.86	-.65	104	.52	-.65	103.20	.52

Test 3
t-test for YEAREVEN (Year Event Took Place)

	Number of Cases	Mean	Standard Deviation	Standard Error
New York	64	85.28	3.55	.44
Toronto	50	82.82	3.91	.55

		Pooled Variance Estimate			Separate Variance Estimate		
F Value	2-Tail Prob.	t Value	Degrees of Freedom	2-Tail Prob.	t Value	Degrees of Freedom	2-Tail Prob.
1.21	.47	3.52	112	.00	3.47	100.16	.00

Test 4
t-test for NUMBEROF (Number of Articles that the Incident Generated)

	Number of Cases	Mean	Standard Deviation	Standard Error
New York	65	3.95	9.41	1.16
Toronto	51	5.43	7.46	1.044

		Pooled Variance Estimate			Separate Variance Estimate		
F Value	2-Tail Prob.	t Value	Degrees of Freedom	2-Tail Prob.	t Value	Degrees of Freedom	2-Tail Prob.
1.59	.09	-.92	114	.36	-.94	113.98	.35

Test 5
t-test for NUOFVICT (Number of Victims in Incident)

	Number of Cases	Mean	Standard Deviation	Standard Error
New York	60	1.43	1.16	.15
Toronto	46	1.07	.33	.05

		Pooled Variance Estimate			Separate Variance Estimate		
F Value	2-Tail Prob.	t Value	Degrees of Freedom	2-Tail Prob.	t Value	Degrees of Freedom	2-Tail Prob.
12.50	.00	2.10	104	.04	2.35	70.94	.02

Test 6
t-test for PUBLICFI (Public Figure Victim)

	Number of Cases	Mean	Standard Deviation	Standard Error
New York	64	1.88	.33	.04
Toronto	50	1.90	.30	.04

			Pooled Variance Estimate			Separate Variance Estimate		
F Value	2-Tail Prob.	t Value	Degrees of Freedom	2-Tail Prob.	t Value	Degrees of Freedom	2-Tail Prob.
1.21	.49	-.41	112	.68	-.42	109.39	.68

Test 7
t-test for AGEOFVIC (Age of Victim)

	Number of Cases	Mean	Standard Deviation	Standard Error
New York	13	20.38	5.67	1.57
Toronto	14	29.93	11.67	3.12

			Pooled Variance Estimate			Separate Variance Estimate		
F Value	2-Tail Prob.	t Value	Degrees of Freedom	2-Tail Prob.	t Value	Degrees of Freedom	2-Tail Prob.
4.25	.017	-2.67	25	.01	-2.73	19.10	.01

Test 8
t-test for NUMOFVIC (Number of Victims)

	Number of Cases	Mean	Standard Deviation	Standard Error
New York	61	1.33	.96	.12
Toronto	46	1.07	.33	.05

			Pooled Variance Estimate			Separate Variance Estimate		
F Value	2-Tail Prob.	t Value	Degrees of Freedom	2-Tail Prob.	t Value	Degrees of Freedom	2-Tail Prob.
8.66	.00	1.78	105	.08	1.99	77.37	.05

Test 9
t-test for NUMOFPOL (Number of Police Officers)

	Number of Cases	Mean	Standard Deviation	Standard Error
New York	46	1.74	1.56	.23
Toronto	36	1.97	1.28	.21

		Pooled Variance Estimate			Separate Variance Estimate		
F Value	2-Tail Prob.	t Value	Degrees of Freedom	2-Tail Prob.	t Value	Degrees of Freedom	2-Tail Prob.
1.49	.23	-.73	80	.47	-.75	79.80	.46

Test 10
t-test for SCOPE (Scope)

	Number of Cases	Mean	Standard Deviation	Standard Error
New York	34	2.38	2.55	.44
Toronto	47	2.68	2.19	.32

		Pooled Variance Estimate			Separate Variance Estimate		
F Value	2-Tail Prob.	t Value	Degrees of Freedom	2-Tail Prob.	t Value	Degrees of Freedom	2-Tail Prob.
1.35	.34	-.57	79	.57	-.55	64.46	.58

Test 11
t-test for ELAPSED (Days Elapsed between First and Last)

	Number of Cases	Mean	Standard Deviation	Standard Error
New York	65	143.34	394.02	48.87
Toronto	51	274.31	510.57	71.49

		Pooled Variance Estimate			Separate Variance Estimate		
F Value	2-Tail Prob.	t Value	Degrees of Freedom	2-Tail Prob.	t Value	Degrees of Freedom	2-Tail Prob.
1.68	.05	-1.56	114	.12	-1.51	91.96	.13

References

Abraham, John D. et al. 1981. "Police Use of Deadly Force: A Toronto Perspective." *Osgoode Hall Law Journal*, Vol. 19, No. 2, pp. 199–236.

Adcock, Thomas Larry. 1984. *Precinct 19*. New York: Berkeley Books.

Albrecht, S. L. and M. Green. 1977. "Attitudes Toward the Police and the Larger Attitude Complex: Implications for Police-Community Relationships." *Criminology*, Vol. 15, pp. 485–494.

Alex, Nicholas. 1976. *New York Cops Talk Back*. New York: John Wiley & Sons.

Alpert, Geoffrey P. and Lorie Fridell. 1992. *Police Vehicles and Firearms: Instruments of Deadly Force*. Prospect Heights, IL: Waveland Press.

Amnesty International. 1996. "United States of America: Police Brutality and Excessive Force in the New York City Police Department." New York: Amnesty International USA.

Anson, Robert Sam. 1975. *Best Intentions: The Education and Killing of Edmund Perry*. New York: Random House.

ARA Consultants. 1985. "Final Report on the Evaluation of the Toronto Ministation." Ottawa: Ministry of the Solicitor General.

Astor, Gerald. 1971. *The New York Cops: An Informal History*. New York: Scribner.

Bachrach, Peter and Morton S. Baratz. 1962. "Two Faces of Power." *American Political Science Review*, Vol. 5, No. 4, December, pp. 947–952.

Baden, Michael M. 1989. *Unnatural Death: Confessions of a Medical Examiner*. New York: Ivy Books.

Baldwin, John. 1992. "Video-Taping Police Interviews with Suspects—An Evaluation." London: Home Office Police Department, Police Research Series Paper No. 1.

Banfield, Edward and Martin Meyerson. 1955. *Politics, Planning and the Public Interest*. New York: Free Press.

Barak, Gregg. 1988. "Newsmaking Criminology: Reflections on the Media, Intellectuals, and Crime." *Justice Quarterly*, Vol. 5, No. 4, pp. 565–587.

Barnes, David M. 1983. *The Draft Riots in New York*. New York: Baker and Goodwin.

Bayley, David H. 1971. "The Police and Political Change in Comparative Perspective." *Law and Society Review*, Vol. 6, No. 1, pp. 91–112.

Bayley, David H. 1979. "Police Function, Structure, and Control in Western Europe and North America." In Norval Morris and Michael Tonry (eds.), *Crime and Justice: An Annual Review of Research*, Vol. 1. Chicago: University of Chicago Press, pp. 109–144.

Bayley, David H. 1985. *Patterns of Policing: A Comparative International Analysis*. New Brunswick, NJ: Rutgers University Press.

Bayley, David H. and Harold Mendelsohn. 1969. *Minorities and the Police*. New York: Free Press.

Beare, Margaret E. 1987. "Selling Policing in Metropolitan Toronto: A Sociological Analysis of Police Rhetoric, 1957–1984." Doctoral dissertation, Columbia University, New York.

Becker, Howard. 1963. *The Outsiders: Studies in the Sociology of Deviance*. London: Free Press.

Bennett, Georgett. 1989. *Crimewarps: The Future of Crime in America* (rev. ed.). New York: Doubleday.

Benson, Paul. 1981. "Political Alienation and Public Satisfaction of Police Services." *Pacific Sociological Review*, Vol. 24, pp. 45–64.

Berelson, Bernard R., Paul Lazersfeld, and William N. McPhee. 1954. *Voting: A Study of Opinion Formation in a Presidential Campaign*. Chicago: University of Chicago Press.

Best, Joel (ed.). 1989. *Images of Issues: Typifying Contemporary Social Problems*. New York: Aldine De Gruyter.

Betcherman, Lita-Rose. 1982. *The Little Band*. Ottawa: Deneau.

Biderman, Albert D., Louise A. Johnson, J. McIntyre, and A. W. Weir. 1967. *Report on a Pilot Study in the District of Columbia on Victimization and Attitudes Toward Law Enforcement*. Washington, DC: U.S. Government Printing Office.

Bittner, Egon. 1970. *The Functions of the Police in Modern Society*. Rockville, MD: National Institute of Mental Health.

Black, Donald J. 1970. "The Production of Crime Rates." *American Sociological Review*, Vol. 35, August, pp. 733–748.

Black, Donald J. and Albert J. Reiss, Jr. 1967. *Studies of Crime and Law Enforcement in Major Metropolitan Areas*, Vol. 2, Field Surveys III. Section I: Patterns of Behavior in Police and Citizen Transactions. Washington, DC: U.S. Government Printing Office.

Blumer, Herbert. 1971. "Social Problems as Collective Behavior." *Social Problems*, Vol. 18, No. 3, Winter, pp. 298–306.

Boggs, Sarah and Sol F. Galliher. 1975. "Evaluating the Police: A Comparison of Black Street and Household Respondents." *Social Problems*, Vol. 22, pp. 393–408.

Bopp, William J. 1971. "The New York City Referendum on Civilian Review." In William J. Bopp and Charles M. Unkovic (eds.), *The Police Rebellion*. Springfield, IL: Charles C. Thomas, pp. 119–134.

Boritch, Helen. 1985. "Making of Toronto the Good." Doctoral dissertation, University of Toronto.

Boritch, Helen and John Hagan. 1987. "Crime and the Changing Forms of Class Control: Policing Public Order in 'Toronto the Good,' 1859–1955." *Social Forces*, Vol. 66, No. 2, pp. 307–355.

Bourne, Paula and John Eisenberg. 1972. *The Law and the Police*. Don Mills, ON: PaperJacks.

Box, Steven and Ken Russel. 1975. "The Politics of Discreditability: Disarming Complaints Against the Police." *Sociological Review*, Vol. 23, No. 2, pp. 315–346.

Brandl, Steven G., James Frank, Robert Worden, and Timothy Bynum. 1994. "Global and Specific Attitudes Toward the Police: Disentangling the Causal Relationship." *Justice Quarterly*, Vol. 2, No. 1, pp. 119–134.

Breed, Warren. 1955. "Social Control in the Newsroom." *Social Forces*, Vol. 33, pp. 326–335.

Brown, Lorne and Caroline Brown. 1978. *An Unauthorized History of the RCMP*. Toronto: James, Lewis and Samuel.

Bruner, Arnold. 1981. "Out of the Closet: A Study of Relations Between the Homosexual Community and the Police." Report to Mayor Arthur Eggelton and the Council of the City of Toronto.

Burns, Tom. 1979. "The Organization of Public Opinion." In James Curran, Michael Gurevitch, and Janet Woolacott et al. (eds.), *Mass Communication and Society*. Beverly Hills, CA: Sage, pp. 44–69.

Carter, David L. 1983. "Hispanic Interaction with the Criminal Justice System in Texas: Expert Attitudes and Perceptions." *Journal of Criminal Justice*, Vol. 11, pp. 213–227.

Carter, Gerald Emmett (Cardinal). 1979. "Report to the Civic Authorities of Metropolitan Toronto and Its Citizens." October 29.

Center for the Research of Criminal Justice (CRCJ). 1977. *The Iron Fist and the Velvet Glove: An Analysis of the US Police*. Berkeley, CA: CRCJ.

Chapman, Brian. 1977. "The Canadian Police: A Survey." *Government and Opposition*, Vol. 12, No. 4, pp. 496–516.

Chibnall, Steve. 1977. *Law and Order News*. London: Tavistock.

Chibnall, Steve. 1981. "The Production of Knowledge by Crime Reporters." In Stanley Cohen and Jock Young (eds.), *The Manufacture of the News*. Beverly Hills, CA: Sage, pp. 75–97.

Christensen Jon, Janet Schmidt, and Joel Henderson. 1982. "The Selling of the Police: Media, Ideology and Crime Control." *Contemporary Crisis*, Vol. 6, No. 3, pp. 227–239.

Clark, John P. 1965. "The Isolation of the Police: A Comparison of the British and American Situations." *Journal of Criminal Law, Criminology and Police Science*, Vol. 56, No. 3, September, pp. 307–319.

Clement, John. 1980. "Review into the Standards and Recruitment Practices of the Metropolitan Toronto Police." Submitted to the Metropolitan Board of Commissioners of Police, March.

Cobb, Roger W. and Charles D. Elder. 1983. *Participation in American Politics: The Dynamics of Agenda Building* (2d ed.). Baltimore: Johns Hopkins University Press.

Converse, Philip. 1964. "The Nature of Belief Systems in Mass Publics." In David Apter (ed.), *Ideology and Discontent*. New York: Free Press, pp. 206–261.

Curtis, Michael. 1970. *Attitudes to Crime and the Police in Toronto. A Report on Some Research Findings.* Toronto: Centre of Criminology, University of Toronto.

Daley, Robert. 1972. *Target Blue.* New York: Delacorte Press.

Daley, Robert. 1978. *Prince of the City.* New York: Berkley Press.

Dean, Dwight. G. 1970. "Alienation and Political Apathy." *Social Forces*, Vol. 38, No. 3, pp. 190–195.

Duncan, Robert B. 1972. "Organizational Climate and Climate for Change in Three Police Departments: Some Preliminary Findings." *Urban Affairs Quarterly*, Vol. 8, No. 2, pp. 205–245.

Dunham, Roger G. and Geoffrey P. Alpert. 1988. "Neighborhood Differences in Attitudes Toward Policing: Evidence for a Mixed Strategy Model of Police in a Multi-Ethnic Setting." *Journal of Criminal Law and Criminology*, Vol. 79, pp. 504–521.

Dunlop, Sheila O. and Denise M. A. Greenway. 1972. *An Examination of the Metropolitan Toronto Police Community Service Officer Program.* Toronto: Centre for Criminology, University of Toronto.

Eckstein, Harry. 1975. "Case Study and Theory in Political Science." In Fred I. Greenstein and Nelson W. Polsby (eds.), *Handbook of Political Science*, Vol. 7. Reading, MA: Addison-Wesley, pp. 79–138.

Edelman, Murray. 1964. *The Symbolic Uses of Politics.* Urbana: University of Illinois Press.

Edelman, Murray. 1971. *Politics as Symbolic Action: Mass Arousal and Quiescence.* Chicago: Markham Publishing Company.

Epstein, Edward. 1974. *News from Nowhere.* New York: Vintage.

Ericson, Richard V., Patricia M. Baranek, and Janet B. L. Chan. 1987. *Visualizing Deviance.* Toronto: University of Toronto Press.

Ericson, Richard V., Patricia M. Baranek, and Janet B. L. Chan. 1989. *Negotiating Control: A Study of News Sources.* Toronto: University of Toronto Press.

Evans, John Perly. 1972. "Blue Power: A Comparative Study of Police Political Behavior." Doctoral dissertation, University of Michigan.

Fagen, Cary. 1984. "Kid-Gloves Commissioner." *Canadian Lawyer*, Vol. 8, No. 5, September, pp. 22–26.

Fainstein, N. I. and S. S. Fainstein. 1974. *Urban Political Movements.* Englewood Cliffs, NJ: Prentice-Hall.

Fink, Stephen, Joel Beak, and Kenneth Tadded. 1971. "Organizational Crisis and Change." *Journal of Applied Behavioral Science*, Vol. 7, No. 1, January/February, pp. 15–37.

Fishman, Mark. 1980. *Manufacturing the News.* Austin: University of Texas Press.

Flanagan, Timothy J. and Michael S. Vaughn. 1995. "Public Opinion About Police Abuse of Force." In William A. Geller and Hans Toch (eds.), *And Justice for All: Understanding and Controlling Police Abuse of Force.* Washington, DC: Police Executive Research Forum, pp. 113–126.

Fleming, Thomas. 1983. "Criminalizing a Marginal Community: The Bawdy House Raids." In Thomas Fleming and L. A. Visano (eds.), *Deviant Designations: Crime, Law and Deviance in Canada.* Toronto: Butterworths, pp. 37–60.

Fogelson, Robert M. 1977. *Big City Police.* Cambridge, MA: Harvard University Press.

Friedenberg, Edgar. 1979. *Deference to Authority: The Case of Canada*. White Plains, NY: M. E. Sharpe.

Fuller, Richard and Richard Myers. 1941a. "Some Aspects of a Theory of Social Problems." *American Sociological Review*, Vol. 6, pp. 24–32.

Fuller, Richard and Richard Myers. 1941b. "The Natural History of a Social Problem." *American Sociological Review*, Vol. 6, pp. 320–328.

Fyfe, James. 1988. "Police Use of Deadly Force." *Justice Quarterly*, Vol. 5, No. 2, June, pp. 165–205.

Galtung, Johan. 1964. "A Structural Theory of Aggression." *Journal of Peace Research*, Vol. 2, pp. 95–119.

Gammage, Allen Z. and Stanley L. Sachs. 1972. *Police Unions*. Springfield, IL: Charles C. Thomas.

Gamson, William A. 1968. *Power and Discontent*. Homewood, IL: Dorsey.

Gamson, William A. and James McEvoy. 1970. "Police Violence and Its Support." *The Annals of the American Academy of Political and Social Science*, Vol. 341, September, pp. 97–110.

Gandy, John Manuel. 1979. *Law Enforcement-Race Relations Committees in Metropolitan Toronto: An Experiment in Police-Citizen Partnership*. Toronto: Social Planning Council of Metro Toronto.

Gans, Herbert J. 1979. *Deciding What's News*. New York: Pantheon.

Garner, Gerald. W. 1984. *Police Meet the Press*. Springfield, IL: Charles C. Thomas.

Garner, Gerald W. 1987. *"Chief, the Reporters Are Here!": The Police Executive's Personal Guide to Press Relations*. Springfield, IL: Charles C. Thomas.

Gaventa, John. 1980. *Power and Powerlessness: Quiescence and Rebellion in an Appalachian Valley*. Urbana: University of Illinois Press.

Geertz, Clifford. 1973. "Thick Description: Toward an Interpretive Theory of Culture." In Clifford Geertz (ed.), *The Interpretation of Culture*. New York: Basic Books, pp. 3–30.

Gibbs, Jack. 1989. *Control: Sociology's Central Notion*. Urbana: University of Illinois Press.

Gitlin, Todd. 1980. *The Whole World Is Watching*. Berkeley: University of California Press.

Glasgow University Media Group. 1976. *Bad News*. London: Routledge and Kegan Paul.

Glasgow University Media Group. 1980. *More Bad News*. London: Routledge and Kegan Paul.

Glass, Gene V. and Kenneth D. Hopkins. 1984. *Statistical Methods in Education and Psychology* (2d ed.). Englewood Cliffs, NJ: Prentice-Hall.

Glazer, Nathan and Daniel P. Moynihan. 1970. *Beyond the Melting Pot* (2d ed.). Cambridge, MA: The MIT Press.

Goffman, Erving. 1959. *The Presentation of Self in Everyday Life*. Garden City, NY: Doubleday.

Goldstein, Herman. 1977. *Policing a Free Society*. Cambridge, MA: Ballinger.

Gourley, G. Douglas. 1953. *Public Relations and the Police*. Springfield, IL: Charles C. Thomas.

Graber, Doris. 1980. *Crime News and the Public*. New York: Praeger.

Grant, Alan. 1980. "The Audio-Visual Taping of Police Interviews with Suspects and Accused Persons by Halton Regional Police Force." Ontario, Canada.

An Evaluation Final Report Prepared for the Law Reform Commission of Canada.

Grodzins, Morton. 1956. *The Loyal and the Disloyal: Social Boundaries of Patriotism and Treason*. Chicago: University of Chicago Press.

Gurr, Ted Robert. 1972. *Polimetrics: An Introduction to Quantitative Macropolitics*. Englewood Cliffs, NJ: Prentice-Hall.

Gusfield, Joseph R. 1963. *Symbolic Crusade: Status Politics and the American Temperance Movement*. Urbana: University of Illinois Press.

Gusfield, Joseph R. 1981. *The Culture of Public Problems: Drinking, Driving, and the Symbolic Order*. Chicago: University of Chicago Press.

Hahn, Harlan 1971. "Ghetto Assessments of Police Protection and Authority." *Law and Society*, Vol. 6, pp. 183–194.

Hall, Stuart et al. 1978. *Policing the Crisis: Mugging, the State, Law and Order*. New York: Holmes & Meier Publishers.

Handler, Joel F. 1978. *Social Movements and the Legal System: A Theory of Law Reform and Social Change*. New York: Academic Press.

Hanson, R. O. and K. M. Slade. 1977. "Altruism Toward a Deviant in City and Small Town." *Journal of Applied Social Psychology*, Vol. 7, No. 3, pp. 272–279.

Harper, Tim. 1983. "Chief 'Ashamed' of Police Raid." *Toronto Star*, September 3, II, p. 1.

Hening, Jeffrey R., Robert L. Lineberry, and Neal A. Miller. 1977. "The Policy Impact of Policy Evaluation: Some Implications of the Kansas City Patrol Experiment." In John Gardiner (ed.), *Public Law and Public Policy*. New York: Praeger, pp. 225–241.

Henshel, Richard. 1976. *Reacting to Social Problems*. Don Mills, ON: Longman Canada.

Henshel, Richard. 1983. *Police Misconduct in Metropolitan Toronto: A Study of Formal Complaints*. Report No. 8, the LaMarsh Research Programme on Violence and Conflict Resolution.

Henshel, Richard. 1990. *Thinking About Social Problems*. Toronto: Harcourt Brace Jovanovich.

Hervey, Juris A. and Peter Feuiile. 1973. *Police Unionism: Power and Impact in Public-Sector Bargaining*. Lexington, MA: Lexington Books.

Hickling-Johnston Ltd. 1982. *Productivity Improvements: Delivery of Cost Efficient Police Services to Metropolitan Toronto Citizens*. Toronto: Hickling-Johnston.

Higgens, Donald J. H. 1977. *Urban Canada: Its Government and Politics*. Toronto: Gage Publishing Ltd.

Hilgartner, Stephen and Charles L. Bosk. 1988. "The Rise and Fall of Social Problems: A Public Arenas Model." *American Journal of Sociology*, Vol. 94, pp. 53–78.

Hopkins, Ernest Jerome. 1931. *Our Lawless Police*. New York: Viking Press.

Hudson, James R. 1971. "Police Review Boards and Police Accountability." *Law and Contemporary Problems*, Vol. 36, Autumn, pp. 515–538.

Hudson, James R. 1972. "Organizational Aspects of Internal and External Review of Police." *Journal of Criminal Law, Criminology and Political Science*, Vol. 63, No. 3, pp. 427–433.

Inglehart, Ronald. 1977. *Silent Revolution: Changing Values and Political Styles among Western Republics*. Princeton, NJ: Princeton University Press.

Jarvis, Eric James. 1979. "Mid-Victorian Toronto: Panic, Policy and Public Response, 1857–1873." Doctoral dissertation, University of Western Ontario.

Jefferis, Eric S., Robert J. Kaminski, Stephen Holmes, and Dena E. Hanley. 1997. "The Effect of a Videotaped Arrest on Public Perceptions of Police Use of Force." *Journal of Criminal Justice*, Vol. 25, No. 5, pp. 381–395.

Jenkins, Craig and Charles Perrow. 1977. "Insurgency of the Powerless." *American Sociological Review*, Vol. 42, No. 2, pp. 249–268.

Johnson, Donald. R. 1981. *The American Law Enforcement: A History*. St. Louis: Forum Press.

Kahn, Ronald. 1975. "Urban Reform and Police Accountability in New York City: 1950–1974." In Robert L. Lineberry and Lovis H. Masotti (eds.), *Urban Problems and Public Policy*. Lexington, MA: D. C. Heath, pp. 107–127.

Kaplan, Harold. 1967. *Urban Political Systems: A Functional Analysis of Metro Toronto*. New York: Columbia University Press.

Kappeler, Victor E., Mark Blumberg, and Gary W. Potter. 1996. *The Mythology of Crime and Criminal Justice* (2d ed.). Prospect Heights, IL: Waveland Press.

Kappeler, Victor, Richard D. Sluder, and Geoffrey P. Alpert. 1998. *Forces of Deviance: Understanding the Dark Side of Policing*. Prospect Heights, IL: Waveland Press.

Kasinksy, Rene G. 1994. "Patrolling the Facts: Media, Cops and Crime." In Gregg Barak (ed.), *Media, Process and Social Construction of Crime*. New York: Garland, pp. 203–234.

Kelman, Herbert and V. Lee Hamilton. 1989. *Crimes of Obedience*. New Haven, CT: Yale University Press.

Klockars, Carl B. 1985. *The Idea of the Police*. Beverly Hills, CA: Sage.

Knapp Commission. 1973. *The Knapp Commission Report on Police Corruption*. New York: Braziller.

Koenig, Daniel J. 1975. "Police Perceptions of Public Respect and Extra-Legal Use of Force: A Reconsideration of Folk Wisdom and Pluralistic Ignorance." *Canadian Journal of Sociology*, Vol. 1, No. 3, pp. 313–324.

Koenig, W. Louis. 1985. "Foreword." In Frank M. Sorrentino, *Ideological Warfare: The FBI's Path Toward Power*. New York: Associated Faculty Press.

Kraska, Peter and Victor Kappeler. 1995. "To Serve and Pursue: Exploring Sexual Violence Against Women." *Justice Quarterly*, Vol. 12, pp. 85–111.

Kraus, Sydney and Dennis Davis. 1980. *The Effects of Mass Communication on Political Behavior*. University Park: Pennsylvania State University.

Lamb, Curt. 1975. *Political Power in Poor Neighborhoods*. New York: John Wiley & Sons.

Lane, Robert. 1959. *Political Life: Why People Get Involved in Politics*. Glencoe, IL: Free Press.

Lasley, J. R. 1994. "The Impact of the Rodney King Incident on Citizen Attitudes Towards Police." *Policing & Society*, Vol. 3, pp. 245–255.

Lasswell, Harold. 1941. "The Garrison State." *American Journal of Sociology*, Vol. 46, pp. 455–468.

Lasswell, Harold. 1962. "The Garrison Hypothesis Today." In Samuel P. Huntington (ed.), *Changing Patterns of Military Politics*. New Year: The Free Press of Glencoe, pp. 51–70.

Lasswell, Harold. 1971. "Fragmentation to Configuration." *Policy Studies*, Vol. 21, No. 4, pp. 439–446.

Leff, Donna R., David L. Protess, and Stephen C. Brooks. 1986. "Crusading Journalism: Changing Public Attitudes and Policy-Making Agendas." *Public Opinion Quarterly*, Vol. 50, pp. 300–315.

Lemert, Edwin. 1951. "Is There a Natural History of Social Problems?" *American Sociological Review*, Vol. 16, pp. 217–233.

Lester, David. 1995. "Officer Attitudes Toward Police Use of Force." In William A. Geller and Hans Toch (eds.), *And Justice For All: Understanding and Controlling Police Use of Force*. Washington, DC: Police Executive Research Forum, pp. 177–185.

Levi, Margaret. 1977. *Police Unionism*. Lexington, MA: Lexington Books.

Lijphart, Arend. 1971. "Comparative Politics and the Comparative Model." *American Political Science Review*, Vol. 65, No. 3, September, pp. 682–693.

Lijphart, Arend. 1975. "The Comparable-Cases Strategy in Comparative Research." *Comparative Political Studies*, Vol. 8, No. 2, July, pp. 158–175.

Liman, Arthur, L. and Max Gitter et al. 1985. "Special Counsel's Report to the Mayor on the Office of the Chief Medical Examiner of the City of New York." New York City, April.

Lipset, Seymour Martin. 1968. *Revolution and Counterrevolution*. New York: Basic Books.

Lipset, Seymour Martin. 1985. "Canada and the United States: The Cultural Dimension." In Charles Doran and John H. Sigler (eds.), *Canada and the United States: Enduring Friendship, Persistant Stress*. Englewood Cliffs, NJ: Prentice-Hall, pp. 109–160.

Lipset, Seymour Martin and Amy Bunger Pool. 1996. "Balancing the Individual and the Community: Canada versus the United States." *The Responsive Community*, Vol. 6, No. 3, Summer, pp. 37–46.

Lipsky, Michael. 1968. "Protest as a Political Resource." *American Political Science Review*, Vol. 62, No. 4, December, pp. 1144–1158.

Lipsky, Michael. 1970. *Protest in City Politics*. Chicago: Rand McNally.

Lowi, Theodore J. 1967. "Machine Politics—Old and New." *Public Interest*, No. 9, Fall, pp. 83–92.

Lukes, Steven. 1974. *Power: A Radical View*. London: Macmillan.

Lundman, Richard J. 1979. "Critical Issues in Criminal Justice." In R. G. Iacovetta and Dae H. Chang (eds.), *Critical Issues in Criminal Justice*. Durham, NC: Carolina Academic Press, pp. 218–229.

Mackey, James. 1985. *I Policed Toronto*. Toronto: Self-published.

Malony, Arthur. 1975. "The Metropolitan Toronto Review of Citizen Police Complaints Procedures." Report to the Metropolitan Board of Commissioners of Police of Toronto, May 12.

Manning, Peter K. 1971. "The Police: Mandate, Strategies, and Appearances." In Jack D. Douglas (ed.), *Crime and Justice in American Society*. New York: Bobbs-Merrill, pp. 149–194.

Manning, Peter K. 1977. *Police Work*. Cambridge, MA: The MIT Press.

Manning, Peter K. 1983. "Organizational Constraints and Semiotics." In Maurice Punch (ed.), *Control in the Police Organization*. Cambridge, MA: The MIT Press, pp. 169–193.

Manning, Peter K. 1985. "The Researcher: An Alien in the Police World." In Arthur Niederhoffer and Abraham Blumberg (eds.), *The Ambivalent Force*. Hinsdale, IL: Dryden Press, pp. 103–121.

Marenin, Otwin. 1990. "The Police and the Coercive Nature of the State." In Edward S. Greenberg and Thomas F. Mayer (eds.), *Changes in the State*. Newbury Park, CA: Sage, pp. 115–130.

Marquis, M. Greg. 1987. "Working Men in Uniform: The Early Twentieth-Century Toronto Police." *Social History*, Vol. 20, No. 40, November, pp. 259–277.

Marx, Gary T. 1981. "Ironies of Social Control—Authorities as Contributors to Deviance through Escalation, Nonenforcement, and Covert Facilitation." *Social Problems*, Vol. 28, No. 3, pp. 221–246.

Marx, Gary T. 1988. *Undercover: Police Surveillance in America*. Berkeley: University of California Press.

Maas, Peter. 1973. *Serpico*. New York: Viking.

McAdam, Doug. 1982. *Political Process and the Development of Black Insurgency, 1930–1970*. Chicago: University of Chicago Press.

McAlary, Mike. 1987. *Buddy Boys*. New York: Charter Books.

McAuliffe, Gerald. 1974. "Police Violence? 9 Toronto Cases Say Yes." *Globe & Mail*, October 15, p. 1.

McClosky, Herbert. 1964. "Consensus and Ideology in American Politics." *American Political Science Review*, Vol. 58, No. 2, June, pp. 361–382.

McElroy, Jerome E., Colleen A. Cosgrove, and Susan Sadd. 1993. *Community Policing: The CPOP in New York*. Thousand Oaks, CA: Sage.

McMahon, Maeve W. and Richard V. Ericson. 1984. *Policing Reform: A Study of the Reform Process and Police Institution in Toronto*. Toronto: Centre of Criminology, University of Toronto.

McQuail, Dennis and Sven Windahl. 1981. *Communication Models For the Study of Mass Communications*. New York: Longman.

Metropolitan Toronto. 1984. *Commissioner of Finance Annual Report of the Commissioner of Finance*, 1957–present.

Metropolitan Toronto Board of Commissioners of Police. Metropolitan Police. *Annual Report[s]*, 1957–present.

Metropolitan Toronto Board of Commissioners of Police. 1970. Report on an Inquiry into Allegations Made Against Certain Members of the Metropolitan Toronto Police. [Judge C. O. Bick, Chair]. Toronto.

Meyer, John Christian, Jr. 1976. "The Nature and Investigation of Police Offenses in the New York City Police Department." Doctoral dissertation. Albany: State University of New York Press.

Milgram, Stanley, 1974. *Obedience to Authority*. London: Harper and Row.

Miller, Wilbur. 1977. *Cops and Bobbies*. Chicago: University of Chicago Press.

Mirande, Alfredo. 1981. "The Chicano and the Law: An Analysis of Community-Police Conflict in the Urban Barrio." *Pacific Sociological Review*, Vol. 24, pp. 65–86.

Monkkonen, Eric H. 1981. *Police in Urban America, 1860–1920*. Cambridge: Cambridge University Press.

Murphy, Patrick V. 1977. *Commissioner: A View from the Top of American Law Enforcement*. New York: Simon and Schuster.

Newfield, Jack and Wayne Barret 1988. *City for Sale*. New York: Harper and Row.

Nie, Norman H., C. Hadlai Hull, Jean G. Jenkins, Karin Steinbrenner, and Dale H. Brent. 1970. *SPSS: Statistical Package for the Social Sciences* (2d ed.). New York: McGraw-Hill.

Nie, Norman H., Sidney Verba, and John R. Petrocick. 1976. *The Changing American Voter*. Cambridge, MA: Harvard University Press.

Niederhoffer, Arthur. 1969. *Behind the Shield*. Garden City, NY: Doubleday and Company.

NYCLU. 1988. "Tompkins Square Park: The First 100 Days." November 19.

NYCLU. 1990. *Police Abuse: The Need for Civilian Investigation and Oversight*. New York: NYCLU.

Ontario. 1972. "Royal Commission of Inquiry in Relation to the Conduct of the Public and the Metropolitan Toronto Police." Report [Judge Ilvio Anthony Vannini, Chair]. Toronto: Queen's Printer.

Ontario. 1975. Royal Commission of Metropolitan Toronto. *Public Safety Services in Metropolitan Toronto* (Background Report). Toronto: Queen's Printer.

Ontario. 1976. "Royal Commission into Metropolitan Toronto Police Practices: Report" (Morand Report). Toronto: Queen's Printer.

Ontario. Offices of the Public Complaints Commissioner. "Annual Report of the Office of the Public Complaints Commissioner," 1981–present.

Ontario. 1983. *Police Act*. Toronto: Queen's Printer, February.

Ontario. 1991. *Ontario Police Services Act*. Toronto: Queen's Printer.

Pierce, H. Bruce. 1986. "Towards Police Brutality Reduction." *Black Scholar*, Vol. 17, No. 3, pp. 49–54.

Pindyck, Robert S. and Daniel L. Rubinfeld. 1981. *Econometric Models and Economic Forecasts* (2d ed.). Toronto: McGraw-Hill.

Pitman, Walter. 1977. "Now Is Not Too Late." Report submitted to the Council of Metropolitan Toronto by the Task Force on Human Relations, November.

Piven, Francis Fox and Richard Cloward. 1977. *Poor People's Movements*. New York: Pantheon.

Piven, Francis Fox and Richard Cloward. 1988. *Why Americans Don't Vote*. New York: Pantheon.

President's Crime Commission. 1967. *The Challenge of Crime in a Free Society*. Washington, DC.

Punch, Maurice (ed.). 1983. *Control in the Police Organization*. Cambridge, MA: The MIT Press.

Radano, Gene. 1968. *Walking the Beat*. New York: World Publishing Co.

Radelet, Louis A. 1977. *The Police and the Community* (2d ed.). Toronto: Collier Macmillan.

Ragin, Charles. 1987. *The Comparative Method*. Berkeley: University of California Press.

Reiner, Robert. 1981. "The Politics of Police Powers." In *Politics and Power No. 4, Law, Police and Justice*. London: Routledge and Kegan Paul.

Reiner, Robert. 1983. "The Politicization of the Police in Britain." In Maurice Punch (ed.), *Control in the Police Organization*. Cambridge, MA: The MIT Press, pp. 126–148.

Reiner, Robert. 1985. *The Politics of the Police*. New York: St. Martin's Press.

Reissman, Leonard. 1972. "The Solution Cycle of Social Problems." *The American Sociologist*, Vol. 7, February, pp. 7–9.

Reuss-Ianni, Elizabeth. 1984. *Two Cultures of Policing*. New Brunswick, NJ: Transaction Publishers.

Ricci, David M. 1984. *The Tragedy of Political Science*. New Haven, CT: Yale University Press.

Richardson, James. 1970. *The New York Police*. New York: Oxford University Press.

Rock, Paul. 1981. "News as Eternal Recurrence." In Stan Cohen and Jock Young (eds.), *The Manufacture of News*. Beverly Hills, CA: Sage, pp. 64–70.

Rogers, Nicholas. 1984. "Serving Toronto the Good: The Development of the City Police Force 1834–1881." In Victor L. Russel (ed.), *Forging a Consensus: Historical Essays on Toronto*. Toronto and Buffalo: Published for the Toronto Sesquicentennial Board by University of Toronto Press, pp. 116–140.

Rogowski, Edward, Louis Gold, and David Abbott. 1971. "The Civilian Review Board Controversy." In Jewel Bellush and Stephen M. David (eds.), *Race and Politics in New York City*. New York: Praeger, pp. 59–97.

Rosen, Steven A. 1981. "Police Harassment of Homosexual Women and Men in New York City." *Columbia Human Rights Review*, Vol. 12, No. 2, pp. 159–190.

Rosenberg, Morris. 1951. "The Meaning of Politics in Mass Society." *Public Opinion Quarterly*, Vol. 15, Spring, pp. 5–15.

Ross, Jeffrey Ian. 1988. "Attributes of Domestic Political Terrorism in Canada, 1960–1985." *Terrorism: An International Journal*, Vol. 11, No. 3, Fall, pp. 213–233.

Ross, Jeffrey Ian. 1992a. "The Outcomes of Public Police Violence: A Neglected Research Agenda." *Police Studies: The International Review of Police Development*, Vol. 15, No. 1, Autumn, pp. 163–183.

Ross, Jeffrey Ian. 1992b. "Contemporary Radical Right-Wing Violence in Canada: A Quantitative Analysis." *Terrorism and Political Violence*, Vol. 4, No. 3, pp. 72–101.

Ross, Jeffrey Ian. 1994a. "Low-Intensity Conflict in the Peaceable Kingdom: The Attributes of International Terrorism in Canada, 1960–1990." *Conflict Quarterly*, Vol. 14, No. 3, Summer, pp. 36–62.

Ross, Jeffrey Ian. 1994b. "The Future of Municipal Police Violence in Advanced Industrialized Democracies: Towards a Structural Causal Model." *Police Studies: The International Review of Police Development*, Vol. 17, No. 2, pp. 1–27.

Ross, Jeffrey Ian. 1995a. "A Process Model of Public Police Violence in Advanced Industrialized Democracies." *Criminal Justice Policy Review*, Vol. 7, No. 1, pp. 67–90.

Ross, Jeffrey Ian. 1995b. "Confronting Community Policing: Minimizing Community Policing as Public Relations." In Peter C. Kratcoski and Duane Dukes (eds.), *Issues in Community Policing*. Cincinnati, OH: Anderson/ACJS, pp. 243–260.

Ross, Jeffrey Ian. (ed.). 1995c. *Violence in Canada: Sociopolitical Perspectives*. Don Mills, ON: Oxford University Press.

Ross, Jeffrey Ian. 1995d. "Violence by Municipal Police in Canada: 1977–1992." In Jeffrey Ian Ross (ed.), *Violence in Canada: Sociopolitical Perspectives*. Don Mills, ON: Oxford University Press, pp. 223–249.

Ross, Jeffrey Ian. 1998. "The Role of the Media in the Creation of Public Police Violence." In Frankie Bailey and Donna Hale (eds.), *Popular Culture, Crime and Justice*. Belmont, CA: West/Wadsworth, pp. 100–110.

Ruchelman, Leonard (ed.). 1973. *Who Rules the Police*. New York: New York University Press.

Ruchelman, Leonard. 1974. *Police Politics: A Comparative Study of Three Cities*. Cambridge, MA: Ballinger Publishing Co.

Rudé, George. 1964. *The Crowd in History*. New York: Wiley.

Sanders, Irwin. 1961. "The Stages of Community Controversy: The Case of Fluoridation." *Journal of Social Issues*, Vol. 17, pp. 55–65.

Sayre, Wallace Stanley and Herbert Kaufman. 1965. *Governing New York City*. New York: Russell Sage Foundation.

Scaglion, Richard and Richard Condon. 1980. "Determinants of Attitudes Toward City Police." *Criminology*, Vol. 17, No. 4, pp. 485–494.

Scaglion, Richard and Richard Condon. 1981. "The Structure of Black and White Attitudes Toward Police." *Human Organization*, Vol. 39, pp. 280–283.

Schlesinger, Philip. 1978. *Putting "Reality" Together: BBC News*. London: Constable.

Shapiro, Fred C. and James W. Sullivan. 1964. *Race Riots, New York*. New York: Thomas Y. Crowell Company.

Sheley John F. and Cindy D. Ashkins. 1981. "Crime, Crime News and Crime Views." *Public Opinion Quarterly*, Vol. 45, No. 4, pp. 492–506.

Sherman, Lawrence W. 1978. *Scandal and Reform: Controlling Police Corruption*. Berkeley: University of California Press.

Sherman, Lawrence W. 1980. "Perspectives on Police and Violence." *Annals of the American Academy of Political and Social Science*, Vol. 452, November, pp. 1–12.

Sherman, Lawrence W. 1983. "Reducing Police Gun Use: Critical Events, Administrative Policy, and Organizational Change." In Marice Punch (ed.), *Control in the Police Organization*. Cambridge, MA: The MIT Press, pp. 98–125.

Simon, Herbert. 1957. *Models of Man*. New York: John Wiley & Sons.

Smith, Paul E. and Richard O. Hawkins. 1973. "Victimization, Types of Citizen-Police Contacts, and Attitudes Toward the Police." *Law and Society Review*, Vol. 6, pp. 135–152.

Spector, Malcolm and John I. Kituse. 1973. "Social Problems: A Re-Formulation." *Social Problems*, Vol. 21, pp. 145–159.

Spector, Malcolm and John I. Kituse. 1987. *Constructing Social Problems*. Hawthorne, NY: Walter de Gruyter.

Stark, Rodney. 1972. *Police Riots*. Belmont, CA: Wadsworth.

Stasiulis, Daiva K. 1989. "Minority Resistance in the Local State: Toronto in the 1970's and 1980's." *Ethnic and Racial Studies*, Vol. 12, No. 1, January, pp. 63–83.

Stoddard, Ellwyn R. 1968. "The 'Informal Code' of Police Deviancy: A Group Approach to 'Blue Coat Crime.' " *Journal of Criminal Law, Criminology and Police Science*, Vol. 59, No. 2, pp. 201–213.

Sullivan, Peggy S., Roger G. Dunham, and Geoffrey P. Alpert. 1987. "Attitude Structures of Different Ethnic and Age Groups Concerning Police." *Journal of Criminal Law and Criminology*, Vol. 78, No. 1, Spring, pp. 177–193.

Sutherland, Harry. 1982. "Track Two." Documentary film. KLS Communications.

Takagi, Paul. 1974. "Garrison State in Democratic Society." *Crime and Social Justice*, Spring/Summer, pp. 27–33.

Thomas, Jocko. 1991. *From Police Headquarters*. Toronto: Stoddart.

Tifft, Larry Lowell. 1975. "Control Systems, Social Bases of Power Exercise in Police Organizations." *Journal of Police Science and Administration*, Vol. 3, No. 1, March, pp. 66–76.

Tobin, Sgt. Theresa C. 1991. Untitled. *Spring 3100*, Vol. 4, No. 3, May/June, p. 5. (Internal publication of the NYPD.)

Torrance, Judy. 1986. *Public Violence in Canada*. Montreal: McGill–Queen's University Press.

Tuch, Steven A. and Ronald Weitzer. 1997. "The Polls-Trends: Racial Differences in Attitudes Toward the Police." *Public Opinion Quarterly*, Vol. 61, pp. 642–663.

Tuchman, Gaye. 1978. *Making News: A Study in the Construction of Reality*. New York: Free Press.

Turk, Austin T. 1976. "Law As a Weapon in Social Conflict." *Social Problems*, Vol. 23, February, pp. 276–291.

United States. 1930–1931. National Commission on Law Observance and Enforcement (Wickersham Commission). *Report on Lawlessness in Law Enforcement*. Washington, DC: U.S. Government Printing Office.

United States. 1947. The President's Commission on Civil Rights. *To Serve These Rights*. New York: Simon and Schuster.

United States. 1967. "President's Commission on Law Enforcement and Administration of Justice, Task Force Report: The Police." Washington, DC: U.S. Government Printing Office.

United States. 1968a. *Report of the National Advisory Commission on Civil Disorders* (Kerner Commission). Washington, DC: The Commission.

United States. 1968b. *Rights in Conflict: The Walker Report*. New York: Bantam.

United States. 1970. *To Establish Justice to Ensure Domestic Tranquility: The Final Report of the National Commission on the Causes and Prevention of Violence* (Eisenhower Commission). London: Bantam.

United States. 1971. Advisory Commission on Intergovernmental Relations. *Police Reform*. Washington, DC: U.S. Government Printing Office.

United States. 1981. Commission on Civil Rights. "Who Is Guarding the Guardians? A Report on Police Practices." Washington, DC: U.S. Commission on Civil Rights.

United States. 1984. "Hearings in New York City on Police Misconduct." Washington, DC: U.S. Government Printing Office (Conyers Commission).

United States. 1997a. "Police Use of Force: Collection of National Data." U.S. Department of Justice, Office of Justice Programs NCJ-165040 (by Lawrence A. Greenfield, Patrick A. Langan, and Steven K. Smith, with the Assistance of Robert J. Kamininski).

United States. 1997b. "Police Use of Excessive Force." Washington, DC: National Institute of Justice/Bureau of Justice Statistics.

Viteritti, Joseph P. 1973. *Police, Politics, and Pluralism in New York City: A Comparative Case Study*. Beverly Hills, CA: Sage.

Voumvakis, Sophia and Richard Ericson. 1984. *News Accounts of Attacks on Women: A Comparison of Three Toronto Newspapers*. Toronto: Centre of Criminology, University of Toronto.

Waegel, William B. 1984. "The Use of Lethal Force by Police: The Effect of Statutory Change." *Crime and Delinquency*, Vol. 30, No. 1, pp. 121–140.

Walker, Daniel. 1968. *Rights in Conflict*. New York: Signet Books.

Watson, Goodwin. 1967. "Resistance to Change." In Goodwin Watson (ed.), *Concepts for Social Change*. Washington, DC: National Training Laboratories, pp. 10–25.

Webster, Jack. 1991. *Copper Jack*. Hamilton: Stoddart Press.

Weitzer, Ron. 1996. "Racial Discrimination in the Criminal Justice System: Findings and Problems in the Literature." *Journal of Criminal Justice*, Vol. 24, pp. 309–322.

Westley, William A. 1970. *Violence and the Police: A Sociological Study of Law, Custom and Morality*. Cambridge, MA: The MIT Press.

White, David and Pat Sheppard. 1981. "Reports on Police Raids on Gay Steambaths." Prepared by Alderman David White and Pat Sheppard. Toronto: Submitted to Toronto City Council (no publisher).

White, Susan O. 1972. "Controlling Police Behavior." In Donald E. J. MacNamara and Marc Riedel (eds.), *Police: Perspectives, Problems, and Prospects*. New York: Praeger, pp. 23–34.

Williams, J. Sherwood, Charles W. Thomas, and B. K. Singh. 1983. "Situational Use of Police Force: Public Reactions." *American Journal of Police*, Vol. 3, No. 1, pp. 37–49.

Wilson, James Q. 1968. *Varieties of Police Behavior: The Management of Law and Order in Eight Communities*. Berkeley: University of California Press.

Wilson, James Q. 1973. *Political Organizations*. New York: Basic Books.

Witte, Rob. 1994. "Comparing State Responses to Racist Violence in Europe: A Model for International Comparative Analysis." In Mark S. Hamm (ed.), *Hate Crime: International Perspectives on Causes and Control*. Cincinnati, OH: ACJS/Anderson, pp. 91–104.

Wolfe, Tom. 1987. *Bonfire of the Vanities*. New York: Farrar, Straus and Giroux.

Woliver, Laura R. 1986. "Sputtering Interests: Ad Hoc, Grass Roots Interest Groups in the United States." Doctoral dissertation, University of Wisconsin, Madison.

Yin, Robert K. 1989. *Case Study Research: Design and Methods*. Newbury Park, CA: Sage.

Zald, Mayer N. and John D. McCarthy (eds.). 1988. *The Dynamics of Social Movements*. Cambridge, MA: Winthrop.

Zemans, Frances Kahn. 1983. "Legal Mobilization: The Neglected Role of Law in the Political System." *American Political Science Review*, Vol. 77, No. 3, pp. 690–703.

Zimmring, Franklin and Gordon Hawkins. 1971. "The Legal Threat as an Instrument of Social Change." *Journal of Social Issues*, Vol. 23, No. 2, pp. 33–48.

Index

About the Author

JEFFREY IAN ROSS is Assistant Professor, Division of Criminology, Criminal Justice and Social Policy, and a Fellow with the Center for Comparative and International Law, University of Baltimore. He has conducted research, written, and lectured on national security, political violence, violent crime, political crime, and policing for over a decade. His work has appeared in many academic journals and books as well as in articles in popular magazines. He is the editor of *Controlling State Crime* (1995), *Violence in Canada: Sociopolitical Perspectives* (1995), *Cutting the Edge: Current Perspectives in Radical/Critical Criminology and Criminal Justice* (Praeger, 1998), and *Varieties of State Crime and Its Control* (2000), and is the author of *The Dynamics of Political Crime* (forthcoming). Ross was a Research Associate at the Center for Comparative Politics at the University of Colorado and at the International Centre for Comparative Criminology at the University of Montreal.